Psychology In Plain English

Dr. Dean Richards
Illustrated by Rebecca Richards

For my wife Andrea, and our
children Matt, Ben, and Rebecca,
sources of most of my practical
experience in psychology as well as
my motivation for most of what I do

CONTENTS

Chapter 1:
Science, Cold Reading, and What's Wrong with the Phrase, "It's Just a Theory."

"Psychology: The theory that the patient will probably get well anyhow, and is certainly a damned fool." Henry Louis Mencken, 1920's American Humorist.

"There is nothing so practical as a good theory." Kurt Lewin, American psychologist.

"Behavioral psychology is the science of pulling habits out of rats." Douglas Busch

"Science replaces private prejudice with publicly verifiable evidence." Richard Dawkins, author of "The Selfish Gene."

"You will never find true happiness. What ya gonna do, cry about it?" Weird Al Yankovic, from the hit song, *"Your Horoscope."*

Science and Common Sense

Let me start by saying that this is a book about the science of psychology. Pretty much everyone knows what psychology is; it's the study of thought and behavior. But this book isn't about just any ol' kind of study of thought and behavior. It's about the

science of thought and behavior. That distinction is essential, but often poorly understood. In fact, there's considerable evidence that Americans, as a group, aren't all that clear about what the word "science," itself means. Most Americans think science is a good thing, a word that makes them think of white lab coats and laboratories and really smart people and modern technology. But, judging from the content of Internet web sites and the callers of talk radio stations and the letters to the editors of newspapers as well as from listening to political discourse, most Americans also would be hard-put to explain just exactly what science is.

Here's an example of what I'm talking about. Just tell people about something that you've read in a book on psychology (like this one), and someone is bound to say, "I think most of that is just common sense." Some may even go so far as to say, "Well, I don't believe in any of this psychology stuff—I think it's a bunch of hokum." (Some might use earthier words than "hokum," but this marks the first time I can remember having the opportunity to use the word "hokum" in a sentence. You've got to allow me **some** fun here.) Other people, on hearing you're learned a new theory while studying psychology, will say, "That sounds okay, but that's just a theory--it hasn't been proven."

All of these comments, and others like them, betray a serious lack of understanding of just what science is, and just what it is not. So I'm going to begin this volume by spending some time explaining what makes the science of psychology the **science** of psychology, how science differs from common sense, and what a theory is (and isn't). We'll also take a look at the relationship between proof and science. In the process, I hope to convince you that scientifically-collected evidence is somewhat more to be relied upon than what dear old Aunt Myrtle always told you about people's behavior based on her many years of working at Target.

What is Science?

Let's start at the very beginning. (I once read a book by science fiction writer Isaac Asimov entitled *The Gods Themselves* (Asimov, 1972) that actually started in the middle. The opening chapter was chapter 6, followed by chapters 1 through 5 and then chapter 7. I found that to be very confusing, and I made a vow from that moment on to always start things at the beginning rather than the middle or the end). So, starting at the beginning, what is science? Many people assume that something is a science if the name for it ends in "-ology." But "-ology" merely means, "the study of," without specifying how that study is being done. Many things ending in "-ology" aren't science at all (such as phrenology, or the practice of predicting personality and other qualities by feeling the bumps on people's heads), and many sciences don't end in "-ology" (chemistry, physics, and astronomy, for example). Psychology itself has branches that are strictly scientific, and others that are considerably less so.

So how do we know the scientific from the nonscientific? How do we know when we're doing science, or reading about it? That has an easy but unsatisfying answer, and a more complex but ultimately more fulfilling one. The easy answer is that you're doing science when you're following the procedures of scientific method. But that's really not much help, is it? It just raises the question, "What is scientific method?"

That's when we get to the more complicated answer. Scientific method is a set of data collection procedures that have been developed over a several hundred year period, procedures designed to collect data as cleanly and accurately as we possibly can. If you're following those procedures, you're doing science, and if you're not, it doesn't matter what you call it, it's not science.

So what advantage is there in following scientific method, and thus doing science? In my experience, the best way to explain scientific method is to contrast it with the very alternative that is often cited by people who are skeptical of science, "common sense." What makes science different from common sense, and why is use of scientific method more likely to lead us to accurate, reliable data than common sense?

We'll begin with the most fundamental difference between science and common sense. Science is **empirical**, whereas common sense often is not. That means that science deals only with things that are observable, issues that can be resolved through some sort of data collection. That observation can be direct, such as things we see with our own eyes, but it also can be indirect, such as when we can observe something by the effects it has on something else. But whether our data collection is direct or indirect, empirical questions are always resolvable by observation. If no amount of observation under any circumstances would resolve a question, the question isn't empirical, and therefore is not in the realm of science. Common sense, though, often deals with things that cannot be resolved through any amount of observation.

So what sorts of things are empirical? Many of the most important, intriguing, and practical questions in the universe. Is the climate of the Earth gradually warming (or worse yet, suddenly warming)? Is there a black hole in the middle of the Milky Way Galaxy? Is the moon made of green cheese? Is it more effective to reason with children or spank them to make them behave? Does your chewing gum lose its flavor on the bedpost overnight? These are all empirical questions. They're questions that can be resolved through one form of observation or another. Note that we aren't required to have actually observed the answer of a question to make it an empirical question, it just has to have the potential of being resolved by observation. You probably don't know, personally, if it's really true that Lizzie Borden took an ax and gave her mother forty whacks, but the question itself is an empirical one. Even though you probably were not in a position to observe the events in question yourself (as you're probably not 120-plus years old), and no one of that time claimed to have directly witnessed the events in question, whether Lizzie really did the deed or not is still an empirical question.

Bear in mind that empirical evidence doesn't have to be direct. We can often resolve empirical questions by looking at the effects a particular event might have. So, for example, if Lizzie's mother was alive one moment and dead of severe axe wounds the next, and we were to observe that no one but Lizzie had access to her during that time period, and that the wounds could not have been self-inflicted, we could fairly confidently state that Lizzy herself did the deed. Such a claim might be bolstered if we added other indirect evidence, such as finding her fingerprints on the ax handle, or discovering a hand-written letter from Lizzie herself confessing not just to the grisly deed described above, but also acknowledging that when this job was neatly done she gave her father forty-one. (By the way, this is just a hypothetical example. In reality, other people besides Lizzy Borden had access to the family household during the time period of the murders of her parents, the handle of the ax used in the murders was never fingerprinted because of a lack of trust in that bit of empirical evidence at the time, and to date, no hand-written confession of matricide or patricide from Ms. Borden has ever surfaced) (Kent, 1992)

Thus far we have determined that empirical questions may or may not have been resolved, and, if resolved, may be resolved by either direct or indirect evidence. That means there are a lot of empirical things in the world. Does that mean that science can potentially solve all our problems? Of course not. Many important things are not empirical in nature. What sorts of things aren't empirical? Metaphysical issues, issues of aesthetics, and disputes involving values and morals, among other things. No amount of observation will determine how many angels can dance on the head of a pin, or whether Monet is a better painter than Van Gogh, or whether it is a better value to spend more time with your children even if it means you can provide less for them, or better to provide more for them even though it means you have less time with them. If you cannot resolve it by some form of direct or indirect observation, it's not in the realm of science.

Many of my students over the years often assume that this means that all religious issues or all claims of the supernatural are non-empirical, and thus outside the realm of science. But that's not the case. When a religious or supernatural claim can be resolved through observation, such a claim enters the realm of the empirical. For example, the issue of whether there are immaterial ghosts is non-empirical, because, by definition, the ghosts are not part of the physical world and cannot be observed. But if you claim those ghosts are having physical effects on the world, such as is the case with poltergeists, that's another story. Poltergeists (literally, "noisy ghosts") supposedly make audible moans and other sounds and throw things. Thus, they can be observed and their existence can be tested empirically. Likewise, if you wish to know if the world exists on the back of a giant turtle (an Ancient Mesopotamian religious belief), or if prayer changes the likelihood that a particular outcome will occur (a belief of many religions), that's the sort of thing that can be tested, because you're making claims about the physical world.

One more issue involving empiricism before we move on. You might have been a bit surprised earlier when I mentioned that not all of psychology is empirical. But there are branches of psychology that make assertions that cannot be verified or disputed by observation of any kind. One example is humanistic psychology, which has as its basic premise that we each construct our own realities. I cannot observe your reality, and you cannot observe mine. If we each construct our own realities, we cannot study other people's realities through observation. Thus, in this most fundamental claim of humanistic psychology, we've left the realm of the empirical and thus the realm of science as well.

Many elements of Freudian psychoanalysis are in the same boat. There's no way of determining empirically whether a particular Freudian dream interpretation is the "right" interpretation, for example. You could generate an infinite number of possible symbols and interpretations for each dream, and no evidence could determine if you had picked the right ones. Nor can we determine empirically if the Freudian constructs of the id, ego, and superego, which play important roles in explaining behavior in his theory, actually exist, because they're hypothetical constructs, not concrete, observable phenomena. (If you're interested in Freud, I discuss him in Chapter 2 of *More Psychology in Plain English,* the next book in this series).

Moving on, besides being empirical, the other important thing science has to be is objective. That is, in collecting our empirical data, we have to make every effort to remove every possible way that we could be affecting the data ourselves by the way we're collecting it. By contrast, common sense is often highly subjective—people generally see what they want to see or what they expect to see, not what's actually there. Ask anyone, for example, if eating sugar makes children hyperactive, and most people will say that this is already a settled issue. Almost every parent of younger children is conscious of this worry, and such parents are constantly restricting their children's enjoyment of sweets for this reason. If you ask people what evidence they have that sugar makes children hyperactive, they all report, "I've seen it! I've seen them eat cookies and doughnuts and candy and bounce off the walls! So I know you have to keep them from eating too much of it."

The trouble with this data collected by casual observers concerning children eating sugar and subsequently bouncing off the walls it that all of it, every bit, is subjective in nature. That is, it was collected by people who expected a certain outcome when they were making their observations. They knew their children were eating sugar, and they expected the children to become more active afterward. As a result, how they viewed children's activity levels might very well have been altered by their expectations. The same level of activity that they were seeing as hyperactive following consumption of cookies might have been judged as less active had the children just had broccoli, celery, or broiled liver for a snack (and we know how much our kids love that broiled liver! Especially broiled liver on a stick!).

If we're collecting such data scientifically, we have to do everything we can to keep such expectations about children's activity levels from affecting our data. That's really not that hard to do in this case. We can do one of two things. We could have machines collect the data rather than people. We could put sensitive motion detectors on the children and allow those objective machines to record actual motion levels after eating celery vs. eating cookies.

Alternatively, we could have someone who has no idea what the children have eaten observe their behavior and make the judgments of the children's activity levels. That latter way of controlling subjectivity, where the observer doesn't know which participants are in which group, is known as doing a *blind study.* By being unaware of which participants are in which experimental group, the experimenter cannot bias his or her observations with his or her expectations, even unconsciously, and the data are thus much more likely to be objective.

(By the way, some people might find themselves slightly jarred by the use of the plural verb, "are," following the word "data" in that previous sentence. Many people don't realize that the word "data" is a plural. The singular form of the word "data" is "datum." Thus, we should always say "the data **are**," not "the data **is**." Unless you're talking about Lieutenant Commander Data from *Startrek: The Next Generation.* Then you'd use singular verbs, because he's only one person, even if his name refers literally to a whole plethora of observations.)

So as our first step in objective data collection of the relationship between children's activity levels and sugar consumption, we'd use machines to collect the data, or do a blind study. But we're not out of the woods yet. There's still another possible source of subjectivity in our little experiment, and that's the children themselves. Pretty much every child in America is aware that sugar is supposed to make him or her a crazed, hyperactive lunatic. Knowing that, these children are very likely to obligingly become more active when they have sugar just because they know they are expected to. The phenomenon of participants in experiments reacting in particular ways because they believe they're supposed to is called *reactivity*, or sometimes *The Hawthorne Effect.* The latter name comes from the Western Electric Plant in Chicago, known as the Hawthorne Works, where this phenomenon was first observed in an experiment back in the 1920's (Adair, 1984).

The Hawthorne Plant story is an illuminating example of some of the problems of doing studies with human beings. Researchers with the company decided to test out whether various changes in work conditions would speed the production of telephone equipment. So they instituted brighter lighting, and productivity went up. Encouraged, they let employees pick their own co-workers, and productivity went up. They added in various other workplace changes, and each time, productivity went up. Having gotten the research results then needed, they removed the favorable work conditions they'd tested, *and productivity went up!*

Puzzled at why productivity would go up when all the working conditions were made worse, they interviewed the employees, and it all became clear. Each time dear old Ma Bell (parent company of Western Electric) changed the working conditions, the workers appreciated the changes and felt obligated, at least temporarily, to work harder in return, because the company was being so nice. And when all the changes were then removed, they concluded that the company must be in trouble and in danger of going broke, possibly because of the costs of all this workplace improvement, so they worked even harder to save it, and to bring back the former working conditions. They changed their behaviors simply because they felt they were expected to in each case, not necessarily because the conditions that were being tested themselves increased productivity (Adair, 1984).

Likewise, it's likely that children are tempted to behave more actively (come to think of it, I believe I said "like crazed, hyperactive lunatics" previously, so we'll stick with that) when they eat sugar, because they know they're supposed to. To keep this sort of reactivity from affecting the outcome in our sugar/hyperactivity study, we need to make sure that the children in our study can't themselves tell if they're eating sugar or not, and thus cannot react just because they're expected to react. One can do this by burying the sugar under other tastes (you can bury a ton of sugar in very sour things like the acids in lemonade, for example). Alternatively, we could use sugar substitutes in the food we give some children and real sugar in the food we give others. If the children don't know who had sugar and who didn't, they can't very well foul up our data by living up to what they think we expect them to do. A study that makes sure that neither the person doing the observations nor the people participating in an experiment know who is in which treatment group is called a *double blind* study. Such studies are considered the gold standard of good data collection.

In clinical psychology, though, double-blind studies sometimes turn out to be very, very hard to do. If we're comparing different types of therapy, how can we administer one type of therapy to one group and another type to another group without the people doing the therapy knowing who got which treatment? And how can we do so without the participants themselves also knowing who is getting which treatment? The answer is that often we can't. Thus, it's often very difficult to completely remove subjectivity from many studies of therapy methods, and as a result it's often very difficult to scientifically compare different psychotherapies.

We also may not be able to do double-blind studies freely when investigating treatments for mental or physical illnesses for ethical reasons. To test if a particular treatment is working, we must compare the results of a group of people receiving the treatment with a group unwittingly being treated with the previous treatment methods, or with people not being treated at all. Chances are that one of these treatments is going to be better than the other. No matter which group our participants end up in and no matter how the new treatment fares compared to the old one or to no treatment, one of your groups is going to be getting the shaft, metaphorically speaking, in that the participants in it won't be getting the best treatment. Is it ethical to assign a group of people who are suffering from illness to ineffective or less effective treatment for the sake of research? It's a difficult question, and it's another reason that true, controlled, double-blind tests of many clinical treatments are often lacking.

Getting back to the dangers of subjective data collection, though, the truth is that we can't trust our casual observations of children's activity levels after consuming sugar, because none of that evidence was collected objectively. But it isn't hard to collect such evidence using a sound double-blind study—all we have to do is get a group of kids, randomly assign them to two different groups, and feed one group a food with massive amounts of sugar while the other group has a food that's sweetened with a convincing sugar substitute. Then we have observers who have no idea who had sugar and who didn't watch the children and record their activity levels, or we fit them with motion detectors and let the detectors measure their activity levels. That's exactly what quite a number of research groups have done over the last 20 years. There have been more than a dozen good, controlled, double-blind studies of the effects of sugar consumption on children's behaviors. So how many of these tightly controlled studies have found that children became more active after consuming sugar than children did after consuming something they thought was sugar but in fact was not? Want to take a guess?

The answer is none. Zero. Zilch. Bupkis. Diddly-squat. None. No controlled double-blind study has ever found that children who consumed sugar became more active than those who didn't. The widespread belief that consumption of sugar causes hyperactivity appears to be completely due to a combination of subjective data collection and reactivity, not due to any real effect (Wolraich, Wilson, & White, 1995).

People are often surprised at hearing this, and yet they shouldn't be. As far as your body is concerned, a carbohydrate is a carbohydrate, whether it's refined granulated sugar (which is mostly sucrose, a combination of fructose and glucose), simple sugars like glucose or fructose themselves, or the starches that make up the bulk of potatoes and pasta. All of these things are treated in the same way once they reach your stomach—the complex sugars and starches are broken into simple sugars, and the whole mess gets dumped into the bloodstream. So if Captain Crunch makes your kid hyper, so should spaghetti, or even turnips and parsnips.

Sometimes people will hear that scientists are investigating a phenomenon such as this one, and they have an enormous good time making fun of the idea. "Everyone already knows the answer to that!" they snort. "Why are they wasting money studying it?" But as you can see, such phenomena are even more important to verify, because often the things that "everyone knows," turn out to be wrong, the product of subjective data collection or wholesale disregard for actual evidence. There was a time when everyone knew that "night air" caused the flu and pneumonia, that baths were bad for one's health, and that touching toads gave you warts.

People who held those beliefs would also have scoffed at the need to investigate them objectively. Yet because of such investigation, we now know these past beliefs are all false. We can open our windows to the glorious summer night air, cuddle our pet toads, and then go have ourselves a nice bath, and I, for one, think this makes the world a much better place. (For more on the value of using double blind studies and the difficulties in using them, see Möller & Broich, 2008).

Which brings us to the second thing you have to do in order to be doing science. In addition to avoiding subjectivity and being as objective as possible, the other thing you have to do if you're following scientific method is to collect all of the data. Every bit of it. Even the data that you don't like, because it doesn't fit your beliefs or your hypotheses. In fact, if we're doing science, we doesn't just *collect* data that doesn't fit our beliefs, we actually go out of our way to *seek* it, something the common sense reasoner pretty much never does. In fact, common sense reasoners generally consciously ignore evidence that doesn't fit what they believe. They do so because they're often arguing with other people and trying to win that argument. When we're arguing to win, our aim in that argument isn't to find the truth (which is our goal in science), it's to rip the arm off of our opponent's argument and beat him to death with it. (I'm speaking metaphorically here. Ripping off real arms also wins arguments, but it's messy and tends to inspire retaliation, incarceration, and lawsuits. Do not try this at home). So when we're arguing to win, we usually marshal the evidence on our side of the argument and emphasize it. Meanwhile, we do our best to sweep the evidence supporting the other side of the argument under the rug and hope no one notices the bulge it makes there.

Note, though, that overlooking relevant data isn't always deliberate. People also unconsciously miss evidence that doesn't fit their beliefs. For one thing, evidence that doesn't fit our beliefs often involves nothing happening when we expected something to happen. Let me illustrate this with a story from my own experience. Years ago, when my children were young, I of course attended a number of PTA meetings. A lot of people bring their kids to PTA meetings because they otherwise wouldn't be able to attend if they had to leave the kids at home. The kids play in the back or outside, the meeting can go on, and everyone benefits. But at this particular meeting, as we were finishing up, this very nice young lady got up and suggested that whoever was bringing the snacks to the next meeting should bring carrots or celery (or possibly broiled liver on a stick, I don't really remember the exact details) and not doughnuts or cookies. "The kids eat those," she said. "And then they get all hyper and it's tough to get them to bed." I glanced behind me and discovered her own two children, who had been snarfing doughnuts not 15 minutes earlier, were not bouncing off the walls, but rather were lying on top each other asleep like a pack of puppies. So I went up to her after the meeting. "I appreciated your remarks about the doughnuts," I said. "Because I'm a 'see the doughnut, eat the doughnut' kind of person. If I didn't see the doughnut, I wouldn't eat the doughnut, and we'd all be better off. But I noticed that you said that sugar made your kids hyper so they couldn't fall asleep, when in fact they just ate doughnuts and zonked right off."

She looked at me with wide, innocent eyes, and then she said the most revealing thing. "Really?" she said. "I hadn't noticed." Bingo! Give that woman a Cupie Doll! Her kids ate sugar and fell asleep, and *she didn't notice*. The most important data in the world, the evidence that something's wrong with her belief, and she doesn't notice it! What a great example to use as the poster child for the dangers of common sense reasoning! But of course there's nothing usual about her in that respect. Most of us don't notice data when nothing happens. And as our beliefs are often about things that happen, not things that don't, we often collect only data that reaffirms our beliefs, and ignore the data that doesn't.

Here's another example. The world abounds with people who believe redheads are hot-tempered. Now of course part of this could be reactivity, as we described above—redheads could just be living up to our expectations by acting passionately because they believe they're supposed to. But even if they aren't doing that, we're unlikely to refute our belief that redheads are hot tempered once we have developed it. Because every time we see a redhead even a bit worked up, it will remind us that redheads are hot-tempered, and we'll add this example to the others we've stored, bolstering our belief. But when we see a redhead being perfectly calm and reasonable despite all provocation, we're not apt to remember that, or even notice it, because *nothing is happening!*

Scientists are aware that we often overlook when nothing happens, or what they call *null evidence.* To counter that problem, they often go out of their way to look for evidence that nothing has happened. That means collecting all the evidence, even the evidence that they're wrong. In fact, in means collecting, especially, the evidence that they're wrong. Most experiments are designed to find evidence opposing what scientists believe will happen rather than to find evidence supporting it. There's a simple reason scientists go out of their way to look for evidence that they're wrong—they, and everyone else, are much more likely to find such evidence if they're looking for it. And if they are wrong, scientists want to know. The last thing in the world they want to do is to stake their reputations on a position only to have others refute their work on the grounds that they've overlooked important data. So here's another important difference between science and common sense: common sense reasoners overlook and conceal evidence that they're wrong, and scientists seek it.

As an example of this, let's take a look at the people who prognosticate. Prognostication comes from the Latin root "pro," which means "before," and "gnost," which means "to know." So prognostication means, literally, "to know ahead of time," including knowing the future, or knowing information about another person before being told. There are quite a few ways to legitimately predict the future. You can, for example, look at what has happened before and predict it will happen again, and often you'll be right. This is the form of reasoning known as induction, and we are all capable of doing it, provided we have some knowledge of what has happened in the past, and how reliably it happens. On the other hand, it's not that impressive to others. It's not the sort of prognostication that gets people to "ooh" and "ahh" (and we all want people to "ooh" and "ahh." It's what gets us up in the mornings).

No, what we're more impressed by is people who purport to know the future through supernatural means, or special means we don't all share. I'm talking about palm readers, and Tarot Card readers, those who cast horoscopes, those who read tea leaves, those who claim to pick up "psychic emanations," and the many other variants of these shenanigans.

There are many, many people who believe, at least to some degree, that some people have supernatural powers, even though objective evidence that this is the case is largely lacking. Why do so many people believe in such a poorly documented phenomenon? We'd have to lay that at the feet of the two issues we've discussed up to this point, subjective observation and hit or miss data collection.

The subjective observation comes in because people want to believe in prognostication. The future is scary and uncertain, and it's hugely reassuring to believe that we can somehow know what it will bring. So we often don't look very hard at those who prognosticate, or look for evidence that they're wrong. When they say something that more or less fits what subsequently happens, we tend to see it as a better fit than it actually is, because we want the reassurance that knowing things beforehand grants us. So the fortune teller tells you "you will meet a tall, dark, handsome stranger soon." If you would happen to crash into an ebony police horse while skateboarding and texting the following day, you might eagerly pronounce the prognostication to have been fulfilled. After all, the horse was tall, dark, quite handsome, and definitely a stranger to you prior to your sudden forceful introduction. The fulfillment of the prediction reassures us that we can rely on the prognosticator for future predictions, easing our fears of the future.

But the hit or miss data collection is the bigger problem in evaluating prognostication. When people are judging whether prognosticators can actually tell the future, they often note only the predictions the prognosticators get right, and they ignore the ones that they get wrong or the ones that don't fit. A psychic, for example, may make thousands of predictions in a lifetime. People readily forget the ones that don't materialize, noting only the few that do. But even a broken clock is right twice a day. To provide evidence of prognostication, the psychic needs to demonstrate not just that he or she can get some predictions right, because we can all do that simply by chance alone. The psychic has to demonstrate that he or she can get more predictions right than any other reasonably bright person who makes no claim to special abilities. But common sense reasoners never recall the missed predictions, they never actually collect the data that would disconfirm the psychic's abilities, they only collect data that confirms it. They're just like the people who think sugar makes kids bounce off the walls, and those who think red heads are hot-tempered. They never collect the data that would disconfirm their beliefs, even when that data is readily available.

At this point, I'd like to take a moment to give all of you a short course in how engage in prognostication (Who knows—if your current gig doesn't work out, you might find a whole new career here). Pretty much all the people who prognosticate or mind read rely on a combination of hot and cold reading to ply their trades. Hot reading is nothing but cheating—it involves finding out information through mundane means and then pretending to have found it out through supernatural means instead. For example, some of these prognosticators and mind readers have live television audiences from which they pick people to "read." These are people who believe in the powers of the host and want to be on the show, so they send for tickets to a taping. The staffs of the prognosticators and mind readers then spring into action. They do Internet searches on people who've applied for tickets, reading obituaries that mention them as survivors, local news stories, social networking sites, and so on. If the person lives in one of the areas where the show has research staff, they send someone out to do a drive by the audience member's home to take notes of everything they see. They might even knock on the person's door in the guise of selling something or of asking for a neighbor who lives down the street, so that they can get a glimpse of the inside of the person's house. Once they get that person they've researched into the studio, it's easy to zero in on them and claim to have extracted such facts from the ether rather than from mundane research. It's like a good magic trick—it looks impressive until you know how it's done.

Cold reading is trickier, but just as effective. There are only a few simple rules to cold reading. 1) Be vague. 2) Be positive. 3) Throw in the advice Mom always gave you. 4) Rely on the person to fill in the gaps, knowing they'll forget that they filled in the information immediately after doing so.

Let's start with being vague. You want to make pronouncements that are vague enough that they can be twisted to fit almost any circumstances, so that they'll fit no matter who you're talking to. For example, I saw a psychic on TV once tell a middle-aged woman, "You're concerned about the health of an older female relative." "Oh, yes," the woman responded excitedly. "My Aunt Matilda! She has the rheumatism something fierce!" The thing is, "You're concerned about the health of an older female relative" is a pretty safe prediction to make, because it's very, very vague. Everyone in the whole world, save possibly for Tarzan the ape man and Mowgli the jungle boy, has older female relatives, even if they're not that close and they haven't seen them in ages. And the word "concerned" is actually a pretty vague term. "Concern" can range in level from being mildly curious to being in a major panic about something. Given the number of people who fit the criterion "older female relative" and the range of interest that fits the category "concerned," it's pretty darned likely you're concerned about the health of at least one older female relative. Being older, they're likely to have some health problem that would cause us concern, and if they don't, we're probably concerned that they might develop such a problem.

Likewise, a prognosticator wouldn't say, "A uncle will leave you more than $15,000 in his will this week," because that's not vague enough. He or she would say, "A surprise financial windfall looms." That way we're being vague about three things—the nature of the windfall, the amount, and the time that it will happen. That vagueness makes it very likely that this prediction will come true for pretty much anyone we might make it to, unless he or she gets run over by a beer truck after leaving your fortune-telling tent on the way to the Liver-on-a-Stick stand. Even then, you the prognosticator could argue that the windfall in question wasn't specifically cited as coming to the beer truck victim, and that instead the windfall was looming for that person's survivors.

The next key to cold reading, after being vague, is to be positive. Tell the folks what they want to hear. My favorite is, "You're far more sensitive than most people realize." Who doesn't want to believe that? Who's going to say, "No, I'm not. I'm an insensitive lout." Even people who aren't sensitive want to believe they're sensitive, and they're far more likely to accept the truth of your statement without question because of it. (Another favorite is, "Most people don't appreciate how hard you work.") The fact that the prognostications of cold readers tend to be overwhelmingly positive is what makes the opening quote from Weird Al Yankovic's *Your Horoscope* humorous. It's the sort of thing cold readers never say. (Such incongruity is often the root of humor—if you're interested in this, there's a discussion of it in Chapter 6 of *More Psychology in Plain English*).

So you tell them what they want to hear, and they'll make it fit because they want it to. Be vague, and your pronouncements are sure to fit. Intersperse those comments with some of that advice your mom always gave you, things like, "Don't trust people who seem to be treating you too nicely—they're probably up to something," and "You can catch more flies with sugar than with vinegar, dear." These aren't actually predictions, but they'll ring true, and make the listener more likely to believe your other statements.

That leaves us one more thing you can count on when you do prognostication. People will connect your vague pronouncements with specific things in their lives, and then they'll voice those specific things so that you can follow up on them. Better yet, later on they'll remember you having made a more specific statement than you did, because that specific connection is how they interpreted what you said when you first heard it.

For example, let's say you're practicing your fortune teller gig, and you give them the old, reliable, "You're concerned about the health of a female relative." Your target is apt to say something like, "Oh, yes! My Aunt Zelda has lumbago! It's been so hard for her to get around since Uncle Clayton died!"

"Her back has bothered her for some time, but doctors haven't helped her" you then say smoothly. It's a pretty safe statement for you as the prognosticator to make. Your victim.....um, I mean, your client, has already admitted that Aunt Zelda has lumbago, which is a vague term for undiagnosed back pain. Had doctors been able to help her, she wouldn't still have it, and the client would be describing what illness Aunt Zelda had in more specific detail than the word "lumbago" provides. So you're safe in your statement that her back is bothering her, and the doctors haven't been able to give her relief. Then your vict...client is apt to say something like, "Oh, yes! When my late Uncle Clayton keeled over, she couldn't even get him out of the sun while she waited for the ambulance!" "His death was a shock to her," you say even more smoothly. It's another safe bet—a loved one suddenly keeling over and dying generally is a bit of a shocker, no matter how old he or she is. "Well, his heart had been weak," your target answers.

Later, talking to friends, your suitable impressed client is likely to say, "He knew all about my Aunt Zelda's lumbago, and he even knew Uncle Clayton died of a heart attack!" But of course you didn't. Your target told you those things. So why does she think that you said them? When two people are collaborating on telling a story, working on a project, or recalling a memory together, they often have a problem with *source monitoring*. That means that they have difficulty remembering who contributed what to the joint product. That's because when I'm speaking, you're picturing what I'm saying, when you're speaking, I'm picturing what you're saying, and it's easy to forget who contributed what part of the picture. I say, "elderly female relative with health concerns," and you immediately tie it to a specific person and picture that person. As humans almost never remember people's exact words when they speak but only pay attention to meaning, it's easy for the client to assume that I mentioned her aunt by name, and her symptoms specifically, especially when I'll pick up that name and symptoms and use them the rest of the discussion.

In sum, then, that's how you can take advantage of the shortcomings of common sense data collection to make your fortune in the world of prognostication. It is those shortcomings in reasoning and data collection that lead to so many people believing in large numbers of things for which evidence is largely lacking.

Now it's time to move on to our last topic in the discussion of data collection using scientific method—reasoning from the data. There are three things scientists do when engaged in reasoning from data. They want to describe the data, predict it, and explain it. Describing data is the main way we get a handle on reams and reams of information. Scientists often aim to describe as much data as they can in as few words as possible. Humans in general have really limited memory capacities with which we consider things, and being able to encompass a lot in a few words is extremely useful. For example, rather than having to remember that if you give Fido a dog treat after he shakes hands with you he'll shake hands more often, and if you give your son a dollar for taking out the trash he'll do it more often, and if you give your employee a raise she'll work harder, you might simply describe all these outcomes and a lot more by saying that organisms who are rewarded for a behavior are more likely to do it again. Thus we can describe a lot of real world behavior in a single descriptive phrase.

Predicting new data is also an extremely cool thing to be able to do. If there's regularity in the world and we figure out the patterns, we can predict what's going to happen next. That means we can be prepared, we can plan, and we can be much safer and more comfortable as a result than if we couldn't predict what's going to happen next. We can't be certain that our prediction will be right—we won't be until the time has passed for our prediction to happen and it either comes out the way we expected or doesn't. But if we can predict anything at all we'll be better off than we were. Take weather prediction, for example. Forecasters aren't always right—sometimes rain comes when they didn't predict it, or doesn't come when they did. But they're right a lot of the time, and that's better than having no inkling of the upcoming weather at all.

That brings us to explaining the data. In scientific terms, an explanation for a collection of data is called a *theory*. Theories propose the mechanisms for why the evidence we've collected came out the way it did. There are two common mistakes people make when they're talking about theories. The first is most commonly made by scientists themselves. Some scientists confuse a theory with data itself, treating theories as if they were facts. No matter how well-supported a theory is, it never becomes a fact. That's simply because it's always possible that there's another explanation for your data out there, and you just haven't thought of it yet. Also, even if a theory is supported by every bit of data you have, there may be data you haven't collected yet that would refute it. Newton's theories of motion were rock-solid when he originally proposed them, fitting all the available data. Only later did new data on the behavior of subatomic particles turn out not to fit his theory, ultimately inspiring quantum mechanics and then string theory.

The other mistake people make about theories is most often made by lay people and common sense reasoners. In this case, though, it's a mistake involving giving theories too little credence. You hear this particular mistake whenever people say, "well, that's just a theory."

People who say, "that's just a theory" are confusing the word "theory" with the word "hypothesis." A hypothesis is simply a possible way things could be. It might be based on experience, or a whim, or just a wild dream you had after a night of drinking, eating liver on a stick, and playing foosball. We often use hypotheses to predict what will happen before we actually collect data. So you can justifiably complain that a hypothesis is "only a hypothesis." But theories don't exist in isolation, the way hypotheses often do. Theories are explanations for data, so every theory has supporting data, and many have reams and reams of supporting data. A theory is never "just a theory."

So how do we judge the goodness of a theory? How do we know if a theory is a good theory? This is fairly simple—a theory is an explanation for a collection of data, so a theory is a good theory if it's based on good data, and if it fits that data well. The better the data and the more of it there is that fits the theory, the better the theory.

We've already talked about how one obtains quality data. You follow scientific method. You set up procedures to make your data collection as objective as possible, and you design your study so that you seek out data that you're wrong. You also record all the data, even the data you don't like (especially the data you don't like). Once you've done these things, and thus have scientifically collected evidence that you can count on, you look at that evidence, and you examine who well the theory fits that evidence. If the theory fits the data you've collected, it's a good theory. If it fits the data better than any other theory we currently have, it's our best theory (at the moment).

Take the Theory of Gravitation. The Theory of Gravitation says that gravity is a fundamental force possessed by all objects with mass, a force that makes such objects attract all other objects with mass. The strength of that force is related to the joint mass of the two objects, and to the square of their distance apart. So is the Theory of Gravitation a good theory? Of course it is. It's a superb theory. We have reams and reams of scientifically-collected data that fits the theory of gravitation, and no evidence that doesn't fit it. Gravity even bends light around the sun, such that stars that shouldn't be visible on the far side of the sun can be seen from Earth fractions of a second before they should be visible. So the Theory of Gravitation is a good theory, because it fits the data, and that data is good data collected by people rigorously following scientific method.

Being based on good data and fitting those data well are the only criteria by which we judge the goodness of a theory. No other factors are involved, especially not whether you like a theory or not. How well you like a theory is an aesthetic issue, and aesthetic issues are outside of the realm of science because they can't be resolved by any amount of observation. Every so often even scientists run across theories they absolutely despise, theories that twist them up inside just to contemplate. In terms of how good the theory is, that doesn't matter in the slightest—the only question is whether the theory is based on good data, and whether it fits that data. If both are true, it's a good theory, whether we like it or find that it jeopardizes everything we live for and hold dear.

Some theories even upset people so much that they want the theory to go away where they don't have to hear it every again. The theory irks them to no end, ties their stomachs into knots, and offends everything they stand for. They'd like it to obligingly disappear. So how do you make a theory go away? Many people immediately say, when asked this question, "You have to find data that doesn't fit the theory," but that's not true. If you find data that doesn't fit the theory, all that will do is demonstrate that the theory is flawed. Such a theory won't go away, because it's still useful for explaining the data it does fit. In fact, every psychology theory in existence has data that doesn't fit it, and some have quite a bit of data that doesn't fit them. But they stay around, because they're still useful for explaining the data that they do fit.

Consider this example from physics. Isaac Newton formulated his three Laws of Motion over three centuries ago. (Well-established and well-supported theories are often called laws, especially when they tend to both describe and predict data. But they remain theories for all that they're called by the more impressive name, because they're still explanations for data.) In the early 20th century, physicist Hendrik Lorentz was able to demonstrate that Newton's Second Law, in particular, does not hold when we start talking about very small objects such as subatomic particles, or we're considering objects moving close to the speed of light. Clearly there are data points that don't fit Newton's Laws. Yet if you take a beginning physics class today, the first thing you'll be taught is Newton's three Laws of Motion. The Laws of Motion don't fit in some situations, but they continue to be taught anyway, because they're extremely useful in describing the movement of objects in most everyday circumstances (for more information, see de Hass-Lorentz, 1957).

Newton's laws, which represent a flawed theory of motion, clearly haven't gone away. They're just too darned useful, and considerably easier to understand than the Lorentz transformations that replaced them or the more elegant Theory of Relativity that later encompassed both. Merely failing to explain some data doesn't make a theory go away. So how do you make a theory go away? There's only one way. You need to find a theory that's better. Once you do, you can trot your new theory out and show it to people, they can then look at how your theory fits the data, and if your theory fits better, it will eclipse the old theory and the old theory will probably be replaced by your new one (Yay!). If your theory fits equally well, it will join the other theory as a competitive theory. If your theory doesn't fit the data as well as the previous theory, it's doomed, even if you like it or its implications better than the previous theory.

There's an interesting principle here, though, one many people who dislike this or that theory don't grasp. Even if you don't like a theory, you can't judge it without first learning the theory. You can't say, "I don't like that theory, so I'm not even going to learn it, and I don't want other people to learn it, either." Because to judge whether a theory is any good, you, personally, have to learn the theory, and then examine how well the data fits it. Otherwise, all you're ever doing is taking someone else's word for whether the theory is any good, and how do you know that person has made a good judgment? Even the brightest people in the world make mistakes—Einstein himself rejected Quantum Mechanics, a theory that now is fundamental to modern physics (Bolles, 2004). The attitude that "I don't have to know the theory because I know it's wrong" makes no logical sense at all. Neither does the attitude, "I don't like the theory so I don't think it should be taught." The only criteria by which we can judge the goodness of a theory is whether the theory fits the data, and we can't judge that *until we have learned the theory.*

24

Wait a minute, you say. What about my beliefs? What if a theory goes against my beliefs? Frankly, that means nothing at all. One's beliefs are totally irrelevant to science. It's not that scientists have no beliefs. Belief is ubiquitous—I've got beliefs, you've got beliefs, we've all got beliefs. Our beliefs give us things to live for, get us up in the morning, give us hope, and keep us going. But our beliefs are limited by two things when it comes to persuading others. The first problem is simply that there are no constraints at all to what you can believe. You might believe that you're sitting comfortably in your home or in your office or uncomfortably on an airport bench, reading a highly stimulating chapter about science, and most folks would agree that this was a reasonable belief. Then again, you might believe that you're twenty-seven miles underground in a cavern having these ideas driven into your head through forced telepathy by an albino walrus while fourteen winged purple elephants fly over your head. Most people would consider you crazy as the proverbial loon in that situation, but you might still believe it, and just as fervently as the rest of us believe we're sitting in comfy chairs (or abysmally uncomfortable ones—I'm not the one who bought your furniture, so don't blame me). Heck, there are probably a good dozen people in the United States this very minute who believe they're Napoleon Bonaparte, and believe it with all the fervency that you believe whoever it is you believe you are. Does that make them Napoleon?

The second limitation to belief is that you can't make anyone believe anything just because you believe it. Oh, it's not that folks don't try. For centuries, people have charged across borders and waved sharp pointy things at other people and ordered them, "believe what we believe." And those people, in turn, have fervently chanted, "I believe, I believe!" But of course they didn't. Internally, they were saying, "I don't really believe, but he's got a sword!" Think about how many times you've told someone else that they were right and you were convinced by their arguments just so they'd shut up and leave you alone. They think they've made you believe, but you know that haven't and they can't, no matter what they threaten you with.

So how do you get people to believe what you believe? Let me illustrate this by telling you about the family pet. My wife and I have perhaps the coolest pet in all of Southern California. We've get a genuine maiden-devouring, fire-breathing invisible dragon living in our garage. Probably the only one left in the world (and I've been looking—I'd like to get a breeding population going. Something to keep me busy when I retire). Quite a pet, right? Beats heck out of your schnauzer or even your pet lobster, you've got to admit.

Wait a minute. You say you don't believe I have an invisible dragon? But all the powers that be say I do! The Mayor himself has signed a proclamation acknowledging I have the only dragon in the city. And the former Governator himself, Arnold Schwarzenegger, even issued a proclamation recognizing I have the only dragon in Collie-fornea! That should make it official, shouldn't it? So now you believe me, don't you?

Gee, you're tough. Well, how about Stephen Hawking? He's a smart guy, right? Developed String Theory and all that? I've got an official letter from Stephen Hawking stating that he believes I have an invisible dragon. You've got to be convinced by Stephen Hawking, right?

Wow, you guys are really tough. Okay, what's it going to take to convince you that I have an invisible dragon. You say you need to see it yourself? Let's review, for a second, the meaning of the word "invisible…."

But that's not what you meant, is it? What you meant is that you want to see maidens disappearing into midair, and fire appearing there. You want to see dragon footprints, and weasels that have been smashed by being trodden on by heavy feet. You want to throw flour in the air and have it land on a dragon shape, you want to be able to feel dragon scales even though you can't see them. You want piles of dragon excrement. (Now there's a pooper-scooper nightmare! Gonna need some Hefty bags for that, not the wimpy ones.) In short, what you want is *evidence*. Observable, empirical evidence. Only evidence will alter your beliefs.

And that's why science deals only in evidence. Evidence doesn't need an advocate, and it doesn't need experts telling us what to think. Evidence stands on its own. People often accuse scientists of following "scientific dogma," and being inflexible, but that's a bum rap. Scientists are the most open-minded people on Earth, because true scientists will go wherever the evidence takes them, whether they like it or not. People in the mass media routinely fail to understand this. They are constantly teasing videos or publishing articles about what "top scientists believe." But, begging your pardon, I don't give a rat's behind what top scientists believe, and neither should you or anyone else. All that really matters is what top scientists have evidence for, because the evidence is all that counts.

The fact that scientists follow the evidence and only the evidence, and that they let the evidence speak for itself is also why I fell in love with science when I was around 9 or 10 (about the same time I fell in love with a whopping big book, but that's a story I'll save for the next chapter). I fell in love with science because scientists didn't treat me like an imbecile who had to be told how to think. Quite the contrary—scientists assumed I could think for myself. They laid out their evidence, described their theories, and then said, "Look at this and judge for yourself. See if you come to any different conclusion than we did." Then they let the evidence speak for itself. Such an attitude is completely fair and open. Have you got a new theory that you think is better than the current one? Trot it on out here and explain it to us. Let us look at your data. But ultimately, your theory is going to have to stand on its own— you can't advocate for it, and you can't force others to adopt it. All you can do is show us the data. If your theory is better, we'll all embrace it. If it isn't, go away and stop bothering us until you have a theory that **is** better. That's why the scientific community operates the most democratic system of information dissemination on Earth, because each theory can be weighed independently by everyone, and no one is being compelled to accept anything.

But one thing no theory will ever be is proven. Not, at least, if we define "proof" as being absolutely certain of the truth of something. Theories are not data, they're explanations for data. There is always the possibility that we will find another, equally good explanation for our data at some point in the future, maybe even two or three equally good explanations (with goodness being judged, of course, by how well the theories fit the data). We might even find a better theory, one that explains not only the data our theory explains, but a bunch of data we haven't collected yet and that our current theory can't explain. Because that possibility exists, we can't say our current theory has been proven, not even with a theory as well-supported as the theory of gravitation. What we can say is that a theory is strongly supported, that a theory fits the data, or that a theory is the best theory we have at the moment.

But that means that we also cannot attack a theory on those grounds. Every time someone says, "Well, that's just a theory, it hasn't been proven," it's all I can do to keep from screaming, "Well, duuuuhhhhhh!" at the top of my lungs and with the maximum of sarcastic expression (and I can be really sarcastic when I want to be. Devastatingly sarcastic. Sarcastic with the turbo button depressed.) You cannot attack a theory for not doing something that theories never claim to do. Claiming that theories are somehow diminished because they haven't been proven is no more valid than complaining that they don't whiten, brighten, reduce waxy yellow buildup, prevent static cling, bring on world peace, or prepare delicious liver on a stick.

It's time to move on to the content of this volume, though, so that's the end of my rant on scientific method, theories, and common sense. The remaining eleven chapters in this volume are about the science of psychology. They discuss hard evidence collected using scientific method, theories that are good theories because they fit that hard evidence, and practical implications of that evidence and those theories. Whether you laud, deplore, believe, or denounce these theories with all your heart and soul is up to you. I provide the data, you do with it what you want. I'm confident you will accept most of it, though, because my psychic powers tell me that you've had your struggles, but you're smarter than most people, and have powers that your friends don't even realize you have. Don't fret, you'll surprise them all someday. Just don't take any wooden nickels. Also, you will meet a tall, dark, attractive stranger while texting and riding your skateboard…

References

Adair, G. (1984). The Hawthorne effect: A reconsideration of the methodological artifact. *Journal of Applied Psychology,* 69 (2), 334-345.

Asimov, I. (1972) The gods themselves. New York: Doubleday.

Berra, T. M. (2008). Charles Darwin: the concise story of an extraordinary man. Baltimore: Johns Hopkins University Press.

Bolles, E. B. (2004). Einstein defiant: genius vs. genius in the quantum revolution. Washington: John Henry Press.

de Haas-Lorentz, G. L. (1957) *H. A. Lorentz, impressions of his life and work.* Amsterdam: North Holland Publishing.

Kent, David. (1992). Forty whacks: New evidence in the life and legend of lizzie borden. Emmaus, PA: Rodale Press.

Möller, H. J., & Broich, K. (2008). Principle standards and problems regarding proof of efficacy in clinical psychopharmacology. *European archives of psychiatry and neuroscience,* 260 (1), 3-16.

Wolraich, Mark L., Wilson, David B., and White, J. Wade (1995). The effect of sugar on behavior or cognition in children: A meta-analysis. *Journal of the American Medical Association*, 274(20), *1617-1621.*

Chapter 2: Linguistic Superstition

*"When **I** use a word,' Humpty Dumpty said in rather a scornful tone, `it means just what I choose it to mean -- neither more nor less.'*

`The question is,' said Alice, `whether you CAN make words mean so many different things.'

`The question is,' said Humpty Dumpty, `which is to be master - - that's all."

(Lewis Carroll, *Through the Looking Glass and What Alice Found There*, 1871)

Back when I was in fourth grade (a time much more distant than I'd like to admit), I was seated for a time in the middle of a row by the wall. Right in the middle of that wall, right beside my chair, was a group of reference books, including the biggest book that, up to that point, I'd ever seen. It was *The Random House Dictionary of the English Language, the Unabridged Edition*, (Stein, & Urdang, (Eds.) 1966) and it was brand new. Shortly afterward, on a day when I'd completed the tasks the teacher had assigned to us, I reached over on impulse, pulled the twelve-pound volume off the shelf with both hands, almost dropped it, and opened it on my desk. And fell in love.

The first thing I did was look up all the dirty words I could think of (I was a ten-year-old boy, after all). To my surprise, many of the ones I sought were there, in stark black and white, along with neat notes describing their languages of origin and with examples of their use in sentences. One of those words is of particular note, because it inspired much of what followed, things that are relevant to my topic in this chapter. That word was "crap."

I can sense the feeling of anticlimax in all of you already. Although mildly offensive to some, the word "crap" isn't that bad a word, not really, and it's very expressive, especially when used in sentences such as "get your crap out of my room!" when shouted by an angry older brother. The reason I'm bringing up the word now is that the word "crap" was instrumental in sparking my interest in the origins and evolution of language.

I was aware of the word in two separate contexts prior to opening the dictionary. The more common one in my life (I had not just one but two older brothers) was the one I cited above, when "crap" is used to refer to things that are worthless in one way or another. That usage of "crap" originated from the Middle English word "crappe," which originally referred to the chaff of wheat, and few things in the world are more worthless than wheat chaff. That word, "crappe," then evolved into two separate words. When used to refer to the light, insubstantial husks of grains, the word gradually changed in pronunciation to "chaff." Yet the original pronunciation didn't disappear – it shifted slightly in meaning, to encompass things that are not just useless but unwanted and perhaps even disgusting in nature. Although it was all "crappe," "chaff" is light, airy, and useless but probably relatively clean, and "crap" isn't necessarily light and airy, and is not just useless but unwanted and probably disgusting (Stein, & Urdang, (Eds.) 1966). So one word had become two, and that was interesting.

But I knew, even back then, of a second use of the word "crap," in the context of a game I'd seen played on *The Phil Silvers Show*, a game played with dice that was called "craps." I even knew that if you rolled the wrong combination of dice in that game, you could "crap out," losing your money. Up to the point in my life when I first dragged that big dictionary from the shelf to my desk, I assumed that the game of craps was named after the fact that if you rolled crap, you lost, or crapped out. It made perfect sense. It was also completely wrong.

The second meaning of the word crap actually comes from another pathway entirely. In the most common form of craps, an initial roll of seven or eleven wins, a roll of two, three or twelve loses, and a roll of four, five, six, eight, nine, or ten requires you to roll until you get that number again without rolling a seven. Craps was a game played by seagoing people going back to ancient times. The twin single dots of a pair of ones, resulting in a roll of two and an immediate loss, resembled the separated eyes of crabs, and that name quickly was applied to rolling a two (rolling "crabs" and thus "crabbing out') and then to the whole game itself (Stein, & Urdang, (Eds.) 1966). Then the "b" sound became a "p" simply because the latter consonant is a lot easier to say, especially in the plural form of the word.

Thus, while the Middle English word "crappe" was splitting into two separate words, "crap" and "chaff" to express slightly different meanings which had originally been united under one word, the word "crabs" shifted to "craps," and people began to "crap out" when losing a round of the game. One word evolved into two because of a need for divergent meanings; at the same time a separate meaning converged and made two previously separate words into one spelling and pronunciation.

I was seized with a revelation. Words changed! Meanings converged and diverged at the whim of users. Some words acquired more uses. Some words split into two, each with fewer meanings. And all of them were listed in this wondrous, huge, ridiculously heavy book! The dictionary wasn't just a place to look up words you didn't know, or to look up spellings (provided you could spell the word well enough to look it up). It was a history of language, and, consequently, a history of human experience. I spent many happy hours that year pouring over words and their histories, searching for the words with the most meanings, the words whose meanings had changed the most, and a plethora of other bizarre word questions that momentarily teased my teeny ten-year-old mind.

Later, I was to discover that there exist among us people who have made a career out of writing long, complex blogs and newspaper columns discussing not just the origins of words but declaiming the right and wrong uses of language. They use many, many words of their own telling us that particular people, most especially modern day teenagers and those they consider "the great unwashed public," are using particular words incorrectly. This is especially likely when it comes to slang, but protests also pop up for everyday, mundane words. "You can't say 'he aggravates me," they say, their noses sharply in the air. "You have to say, 'he irritates me.' 'Aggravate' means 'to make worse.' 'Irritate' means 'to bother.' You aggravate a condition or illness, but irritate a person." Likewise, they say, with sanctimony ringing in their voices, "You can't say, 'this committee is comprised of 13 individuals.' The whole comprises the parts, so you have to say 'this committee comprises 13 individuals.'"

These are the language police, and like the Highway Patrol hiding on stretches of lonely road, they're there to save us from the folly of being ourselves. Many are on a holy crusade, fighting a losing battle against "improper usage." And they take every example of usage heresy that they hear as clear evidence that the world is going to Hell in a hand basket, with misuse of language as the propelling force.

The people who are protesting the improper use of language terms are making a critical and, when you look at it carefully, very likely mistaken assumption. They're assuming that words have set meanings in and of themselves, meanings that exist irrespective of who is using the words. Those meanings are denoted the "right" meanings, and any deviation from them would be improper usage. Professional linguists have a phrase they use to refer to this belief. They call it "linguistic superstition" (Gray, 1991).

So what is linguistic superstition, and what does it have to do with chaff, craps, and the price of liver on a stick? Do words have meanings separate from humans using them? I'll address that issue in a moment. But we'll first have to take a bit of a detour, and consider another human phenomenon – a phenomenon referred to by social psychologists as "cognitive economizing," or "the principle of least effort" (Tolman, 1932).

Human beings are bright, especially compared to other animals – really, really bright. (Try not to what they call "the big head" in many rural parts of the country – I'm talking about in comparison to the average eggplant, earthworm or mussel. That's not a very high bar, after all). We're bright, and we're capable of the most remarkable abilities to think, to juggle information, and to employ all sorts of feats of mental gymnastics. But that doesn't mean that we go out of our way to use those abilities. Actually, it's quite the reverse. We appear to try to avoid thinking any harder than we have to whenever possible, unless struck by a sudden whim to exercise our brains, and such whims are as short lived as a reality show marriage. Thinking is effortful, tiring, and often frustrating as well. And when things are effortful, tiring, and frustrating, we'll generally avoid them as much as possible. So frequently we simplify the process of our thinking as much as possible, using shortcuts when we can, cribbing from past memories if we have them, and ignoring minor details and nuances if they complicate the task.

This usage of shortcuts and oversimplifications is called "cognitive economizing," and our tendency to take the easy way out the "principle of least effort." Cognitive economizing pops up everywhere. We do things the way we've always done them whenever possible rather than work out new methods. We use the same greetings and farewells day after day rather than think up new things to say. We even have the same conversations with people over and over again. We run on autopilot whenever possible. We also see this type of cognitive economizing in the construction and usage of language itself.

For example, frequently used words and phrases get shortened as much as possible. The original word for a flying machine, "aeroplane," was shortened to "airplane," a term with one less syllable, and then just to "plane." That noisier, less efficient, but more versatile rotary winged craft, originally a "helicopter," became just a "copter," or a "chopper." And the process of cooking food in a "microwave oven," became simply to "microwave," and then to "nuke." The most commonly used words in the English language are often the shortest – for example, generic words of being, (be, is, was, were), words of doing (do, did, does, done), and words of having (has, had, have) are all single syllables.

We cognitively economize in other ways, too. One of these ways is to combine multiple, related meanings into single words. Because of this, it's not at all uncommon for words we already know to be used for new purposes. They take up the job where new words might have been needed instead. This saves us the trouble of coming up with new words and keeps the number of words we really need to know down to a manageable level. Most words have several meanings, and some have ridiculous numbers of meanings. As I originally discovered as a bored 10-year-old, the word "run," has no fewer than 172 separate definitions in the unabridged version of *The Random House Dictionary of the English Language* (Stein, & Urdang, (Eds.) 1966). Run can mean "to go quickly by moving the legs more rapidly than at a walk," "to charge as on a charge account," "a sequence of cards in a given suit," or any of 169 other things. The range of meanings for "run" is quite wide indeed. You might wonder how a word acquires such a range of meanings, but it's usually a gradual process. The word acquires a meaning similar to the original one, then it acquires meanings similar to the new ones, and then those meanings inspire more, similar meanings, and the meanings gradually diverge. Some of the meanings are very different from others, but they all related to other meanings which related to other meanings, until they're all at least sort of connected. We could use different words for each of those meanings, but then we'd need to know all those different words. Thus it's easier to use the same word for a variety of different, but related meanings.

So if I were to ask you, "What does 'run' mean?" I bet the question gives you pause. It's not that you don't know what the word run means – it's that you know too many things it means. And I haven't given you enough information in that single sentence for you to pin down which of the meanings I'm using. I haven't used the word. Without the context of usage, the word could mean any of the 172 possibilities listed in the Random House dictionary. Linguists say this problem of not knowing, out of context, what a word means, arises because we're assuming words have intrinsic meanings. But that just isn't the case. Words are merely arbitrary sounds, signs, or arrangements of letters. They didn't mean anything originally, before they were used by humans, and they don't mean anything now, either, even though they've been used by humans for particular purposes in the past. Linguists argue words don't mean anything except when they are being used by a human to communicate to another human. Then they mean whatever the user intends for them to mean.

Which makes the Humpty-Dumpty quote at the start of this chapter considerably more profound than the average child or adult realizes upon reading it for the first time. Humpty isn't saying that words have no meaning – he's saying they acquire meaning when they're used, and that meaning is whatever the user was trying to say. Now it's true that if the word is used in a way that's unexpected by the target of the speaker, odds are pretty good the listener won't understand the user's meaning, and that will reduce the chances the speaker will be understood. If no understanding occurs, we could indeed argue that the word was being used wrongly. But if the speaker and the listener both agree on the meaning of the word, well, then, the word acquires that meaning upon being used to communicate.

The essence of the argument concerning linguistic superstition, then, is that words have no existence separate from the existence of human beings. They acquire meaning only when humans agree upon that meaning. But many people don't realize this, because words have been in use for so long and by so many people that we start thinking in terms of the words having a set, specific meaning, and we become resistant to that meaning being changed. If someone uses a term differently, we decry it, even if the people using it are communicating perfectly well. And thus, we have the source of linguistic superstition and all the consequences that arise from it.

So why do we have the impression that words have meanings that are set and permanent? Because when we use them in context, we, and the people we are communicating with, know exactly which of the many meanings and nuances of meaning of the word we intend to mean. Do the four, five, six, and seven of hearts make a "run" in gin rummy? Of course. Does the sap "run" in the springtime in Vermont? Indubitably. Do you know what I mean if I say I'm going to "run" a tab at the bar, or "run" over to the store, or that the movie had a good "run?" Of course you do, with no doubt in your mind. I don't have to "run" over the meanings in your mind again, you don't have to "run" to an expert to understand me, and you're probably thinking right now that I've "run" this particular example into the ground. Regardless, in each case the meanings are clear.

Even in the case of words that are more abstract, words like "love," or "truth," are clearly defined when we use them, allowing listeners to know which of many theoretically possible uses are what is meant in this case. If I say you love free-verse poetry, you love your dog, you love pizza, you love your significant other, and you'd love it if I'd get to the point, I mean something different with each usage, but each usage is perfectly clear.

I mention this point, because it's common for teenagers (at least, somewhat awkward, nerdy teenagers, a group that once included me), often at parties in the wee hours of the morning, to ponder the deep questions of the universe. Among the deep questions that often come up in these sleep-deprivation-addled conversations are questions of meaning. "What is love? What is truth?" we asked each other as teens, and teens still ask each other today. In response, kids today, just as we did then, puzzle for a bit in joint confusion (confusion sometimes helped along by the fact that it is, after all, 2 in the morning), and conclude, "I don't know. I guess no one knows what love and truth are. It's a mystery."

In a sense that conclusion is correct. In that context, at that time, the meanings of love and truth are mysteries. But they weren't real mysteries. They were what professors who teach critical thinking call "pseudomysteries" -- mysteries that come about just because of games with language (Gray, 1991). When we ask, "What is truth?" or "What is love?" we aren't actually using the words, we're just laying them out there without using them and asking what they mean. As a result, we are in no more position to answer what they mean than we could have if we had we asked, "what does 'run' mean?" When we don't use a word in context to communicate something, it doesn't mean anything. To think that it does is to be caught up in the pitfall trap of linguistic superstition. The meanings of the words are only a mystery because, in our wide-eyed, callow, overbearing youth, we are trying to divine the meaning of a word that isn't currently being used, never realizing the futility of that exercise.

All sorts of things follow from the proposition that words acquire meaning only when they're used. For example, one corollary is that if humans start using words differently from before, the words will acquire new meanings as a result. Are these new meanings wrong? Many would argue that this is indeed the case, and those people spend a great deal of time teaching us the "right" way to use the words. Are they wrong for doing so, or are the people shifting word meanings the ones who are wrong?

I'm tempted to say that it depends by what you mean by "wrong." Oh, what the heck, I will say that. On the side of the language police, if you use a word in a way that no one else does, you won't be understood, and there won't be communication, and that's wrong because communication was the only reason for using the word to start with. But on the side of the common person and the proportion of us who are somewhat more mellow and laid back, if the person you are talking to knows what you mean by the word, then communication has taken place, and by that standard the word was right for the situation.

So if enough of the population, or at least enough of the people you're talking to, understand your new usage of the word, then that's what the word means, regardless of what it meant in the past. Words have migrated and changed in meaning continuously in every living language of the world throughout history. According to the Oxford English Dictionary (Simpson & Weiner, 1989) , the term "congress," originally meant "coming together," and the term was often used in earliest times as a euphemism for sexual intercourse. That usage became increasingly uncommon in the 1700's, and reference to groups of people meeting to engage in discussion became rather more common. After the several Continental Congresses had met, and the Constitution established a ruling body of that name, that original, more bawdy usage of "congress" became so rare few people today realize the word could have any other meaning. Many senators today would probably bridle at the suggestion that the word "congress" has this rather R-rated meaning, and decry it as a "wrong" use of the word. Yet if I were to tell you that it is true that the Senator and the exotic dancer engaged in congress in his or her Washington office, I'm pretty sure you'd understand what it was they did perfectly without me having to spell it out any further.

As a professor of psychology and a representative of an educational establishment promoting clear communication, I tried for many years to stem the tide of the shift in word usage. I repeatedly explained on student papers that "the whole **comprises** the parts, the parts **compose** the whole." I ranted to many and sundry that the word "unique" means "one of a kind," and thus is not capable of gradations. You can't be "very unique," or "rather unique" – you're either one of a kind or you're not. It's like being pregnant, gone, or dead.

I reserved special disdain for people who said, "I could care less." "You don't mean that," I'd say. "You mean the opposite of that, in fact. If you say you could care less, it means that you care at least some, or it wouldn't be possible for you to care less. What you're trying to say is that you couldn't care less!" It was enough to make me pull my hair out in exasperation, possibly one of the reasons I'm getting rather short of hair these days.

How successful have I been in those protestations? Ever try to bail a boat with a sieve? Push water uphill? Keep the sun from rising in the morning? Fighting drift in the language is a similarly effective endeavor. If the tide is coming in, wearing yourself out flailing about with a bucket won't hold it back. In fact, sooner or later you get the overwhelming urge to just turn over on your back and float along with the tide. If enough people in the world insist on using a word a certain way, then the word acquires that meaning. Nothing horrible happens. The world keeps spinning on its axis, and we all go on with our lives. Much as I hate hearing an athlete described as "very unique," I can't say that I don't know what the person is saying or trying to communicate. If the word "unique" shifts to meaning something more in the neighborhood of "special," rather than "one of a kind," well, that's just the way it is. If I persist in complaining that the word should be used some other way because that's how it used to be used, the truth is that I'm just being unnecessarily difficult. It's just another English word expanding in usage to be more useful to us, cognitive economizing at work once again. Like the word "run," the word "unique" becomes broader and more useful, and yet because of context we're still communicating which of the possibilities we mean. On the other hand, that then leaves us without a word meaning, specifically, "one of a kind," and that could pose a problem, perhaps even requiring the coining of a new word at some point.

So how do we know which of the meanings of the words "run," or "love" other speakers are referring to when they use the words they use? The words narrow it down some, it's true, but how do we figure out the exact thing denoted by the word? The truth is, the actual words we use in communication are only a small part of the communication itself. Context of the communication, including the setting, the surroundings, and, most importantly, what has been said before, carries a big chunk of the rest. Considering the fact that we are discussing playing gin rummy or pinochle, my complaint that my father keeps getting run after run is crystal clear. Considering the fact that we are talking about the man or woman you are thinking about marrying, the question, "do you love him/her?" is completely understandable, or at least close enough to completely understandable for government work. The context, including what was said before, tells you what meaning to use.

Consider the following paragraph:
If he could break the lock, he'd be able to escape. But he'd have to time it just right, and it would take every fiber of his strength. He knew, deep within himself, that it wouldn't pay to jump the gun – too many people depended upon his actions in the next few minutes. Yet he was sure he could do it—he was strong enough, he'd prepared for so long. If he timed it just right, it was all a matter of the right pressure in the right direction. Now! The motions he'd practiced in training flowed fluidly, and he felt the

lock give way. He ducked, rolled, and was free! Scrambling backwards, he took in his surroundings and immediately began planning how he could turn the tables on his long time opponent.

The words of the above paragraph are English, presumably a language you're familiar with. Yet I bet you're entertaining a certain amount of ambiguity in your mind concerning just what was going on. Take a simple word like "lock." What did I mean when I talked about him breaking the lock? The word is clearly a noun, describing a thing, but what sort of thing? What sort of lock did you picture when reading the story? And when I talked about the motions that he'd practiced in training, what sort of motions was I talking about, and what sort of training? Where did he get that training, who trained him, and what were they wearing when it happened? How did you picture the "long time opponent" I referred to? Is the opponent a man, a woman, a German Shepherd? If the opponent was a person, what was he or she wearing? What sort of actions was our protagonist planning when he began preparing to turn the tables?

You may have had ideas in your mind of a very specific sort when you read the passage, but I doubt you all had the same things in mind. As I gave you no context for the story, you had to draw up your own context, and likely different people came up with different contexts. Now consider the difference if I had given the passage a title before your commenced reading it. What if I told you the story was titled, "The Wrestling Match," or "Escape from Stalag 11," or "The Knight Errant?" Go ahead and read the story again with each of these titles in mind and see how it changes the meaning of my words.

Context is a big part of the meaning of the story, because "lock," like "run," has multiple meanings. It could be a physical hold of great strength, a mechanical device buried in a door, a separate clasp opened and closed with a key, or even a sure-fire bet if we were talking about a football game. We may not know which meaning the speaker is referencing out of context. But, honestly, whenever do we reference the word out of context? Used in context, we usually know precisely what the storyteller means. Charles Lutwidge Dodgson, the British mathematician known more popularly by the pen name Lewis Carroll and the author of the Humpty-Dumpty quote above, was a man gifted with an early and especially clear understanding of the fluidity of language and also possessed with a clear understanding of the folly of linguistic superstition. (Whatever happened to naming boys Lutwidge, by the way? I haven't met a Lutwidge since, well, ever.) The eldest of 11 children, Dodgson apparently became gifted at storytelling in part by practicing on younger siblings and cousins. By the time he was a young man, he was regularly putting together a publication of his own, *Mischmasch*, for the amusement of his relatives, in which he played with language and tried out various little stories that were later incorporated into his two Alice books, *Alice in Wonderland* and *Through the Looking Glass and What Alice Found There* (Carroll, 1871).

In his writings, Dodgson's position on Humpty-Dumpty's question of whether we should be the slaves of or the masters of language was clear – he saw humans as the masters and language as slave to our whims of communication. Inventor of an early form of Scrabble, Dodgson saw words as tools. He also was fond of creating anacrostic poems, poems where the first letter of each line spelled out the names of friends and acquaintances (an untitled poem near the end of *Through the Looking Glass* spells out "Alice Pleasance Liddell," the seven and a half year old girl who was probably the inspiration for the protagonist of the two Alice books). He made language dance to his own tune.

Yet Dodgson grew up in an era when British schoolchildren were often made slaves to a dead language, Latin. In Dodgson's time, most English schoolboys spent hours laboriously memorizing and conjugating, learning the "right" way to speak Latin and the "right" uses of its words, learning that was often encouraged by a twisting of an ear or a sharp rap of knuckles on the head. English was treated the same way – school children were there to learn to speak it properly – to use the King's English rather than the dialects like Cockney that everyone actually used to communicate. Yet English wasn't and isn't Latin. Latin hadn't been spoken as the everyday language of a living people for more than a thousand years by that point. The exact usage of Latin was embodied in books from which every child in England learned, and there was no danger of an extinct populace changing that proper usage by altering their own use. But English was different-- it was a living language that was evolving and changing as humans changed the way it was used in communicating with each other. Because it was a living language spoken by millions, attempts to keep English fixed and unchanging and to talk about the "right" and "wrong" usages and "right" and "wrong" ways to speak English was a losing proposition. And, as Dodgson knew, it also drained the life, the whimsy, and the joy out of the language. Children struggling to express themselves the "right" way lost their zest for linguistic expression, developed a fear of writing and speaking, and became slaves to the language.

You can see Dodgson's playfulness with language throughout the Alice books. That whimsy is a good part of the enduring pleasure these books give to readers. As Alice drinks and eats things that make her larger and smaller, Dodgson makes the point that such adjectives have no meaning out of context. Whether a human or other object is "big" or "little" depends upon the sizes of the people or objects to which we're comparing them. A dormouse might be small to normal humans, but big and threatening to a much smaller Alice. So is it true that a dormouse is "little?" It depends on Alice's size at the moment, doesn't it?

The most important point that Dodgson makes in terms of mastering language rather than being a slave to it unfolds in his most famous poem, a wonderful masterpiece of whimsical language usage entitled "Jabberwocky." "Jabberwocky" appears in *Through the Looking Glass and What Alice Found There*, in the form of an entry in a book of poetry Alice stumbles across lying on a table soon after passing through the looking glass. The poem, about the hunting and killing of a mythical creature referred to as the Jabberwock, contains quite a number of what Dodgson called "portmanteau words," or words that are invented by combining other words. (The word "portmanteau" is itself a portmanteau word. It's of French origin, a combination of "porter," which in French means "to carry," and "manteau," French for "cloak." Originally, a portmanteau was a servant of the king who carried the king's robes around in a sort of folding trunk in case the king might need them. The word then evolved, as words being used by humans do, until it was used to refer to any sort of suitcase with opening sections, such as the trunk used by a human portmanteau. Then it was stretched by Dodgson to apply to words that resembled the suitcase known as a portmanteau in that they were made of parts.) For aid in the next part of our discussion, I'm going to reprint Jabberwocky here, a process made much easier by the fact that the poem, and the illustration that accompanies it, are both now in the public domain.

Jabberwocky
By Lewis Carroll

`Twas brillig, and the slithy toves
  Did gyre and gimble in the wabe:

All mimsy were the borogoves,
  And the mome raths outgrabe.

"Beware the Jabberwock, my son!
  The jaws that bite, the claws that
catch!
Beware the Jubjub bird, and shun
  The frumious Bandersnatch!"

He took his vorpal sword in hand:
  Long time the manxome foe he
sought --
So rested he by the Tumtum tree,
  And stood awhile in thought.

And, as in uffish thought he stood,
  The Jabberwock, with eyes of flame,
Came whiffling through the tulgey wood,
  And burbled as it came!

One, two! One, two! And through and through
  The vorpal blade went snicker-snack!
He left it dead, and with its head
  He went galumphing back.

"And, has thou slain the Jabberwock?
  Come to my arms, my beamish boy!
O frabjous day! Callooh! Callay!'
  He chortled in his joy.

`Twas brillig, and the slithy toves
  Did gyre and gimble in the wabe;
All mimsy were the borogoves,
  And the mome raths outgrabe.

(Carroll, 1871)

The portmanteau words that Dodgson uses in *Jabberwocky* include such classics as "brillig," "slithy," "whiffling," "galumphing," and "beamish." In the context of the poem, the meaning of the words is at least partially clear to all and often crystal clear, and the poem itself is understandable even though it includes almost two dozen of Dodgson's made-up words. When we're told the boy "went galumphing back," after his triumph, his style of movement is perfectly clear to us—we can just picture his galloping, humping gait. The "slithy toves" that "gyre and gimble in the wabe," are clearly both slippery and lithe, and in our mind's eye we see them twisting and digging in the dying light of afternoon. And who, among us, has not seen our share of beamish boys or experienced frabjous days? The words communicate information, even though, prior to our reading the poem, they were not, to us, words at all.

Modern day portmanteau words include such easily understandable words as "spork," for the plastic spoon-fork combination given out at fast food restaurants, "blog," a shortening of "web log," "breathalyzer," a shortening of "breath analyzer," "dumbfound," a combination of "dumb" and "confound," and hundreds of others. Such words often enter the language easily and quickly, spreading world-wide in days, because they do what Humpty Dumpty suggested they should do. They communicate just what they're supposed to communicate – no more and no less. (Not a bad observation for an egg creature with a penchant for perching precariously on walls).

Can you use language wrongly? Yes, if you're not communicating when you do it. No, if at least the person you're addressing understands you, or if your usage quickly drops into widespread use. Entertainingly, unforgettably, *Jabberwocky* makes Dodgson's point about linguistic superstition. His words are tools, the tools of humans, and he feels free to use them in whatever way he, as a human, wants to use them, and so should we. My realization that words evolved, back there in the 4th grade, was the beginning of my determination to make language my slave rather than my master. It was probably in part nostalgia for that realization that made me go out and buy, as one of my first purchases as a newly minted assistant professor, an unabridged *Random House Dictionary of the English Language* of my very own.

Would I be writing this today if I'd sat in the middle of the 4th grade classroom, perhaps surrounded by congenial, attractive young ladies who found me strangely charming rather than between a phalanx of surly little boys and a wall of shelves holding a whopping big book? Would I have later discovered the *Oxford English Dictionary* (Simpson & Weiner, 1989), and its documentation of even the earliest, most obscure usages of common and uncommon words, if I hadn't been fascinated by that (comparatively) smaller Random House Dictionary? I'll never know; I'm pretty sure you don't care, and I doubt if "what ifs" of this nature merit much pondering. The only really important issue is that when I use these words, you understand just what I intend for them to mean—no more and no less. And I would challenge the language police with this question--what else is language for?

References:

Carroll, L. (1871). *Through the looking glass and what Alice found there.* London: Macmillan and Co.

Carroll, L. (1932). *The rectory umbrella and Mischmasch.* London: Cassell & Co., Ltd.

Gray, W. D. (1991). *Critical thinking about new age ideas.* Pacific Grove, CA: Brooks & Cole.

Simpson, J. A., & Weiner, E. S. C. (1989). The oxford english dictionary (2nd Ed.). Oxford: Clarendon Press.

Stein, J., and Urdang, L. (Eds.) (1966). *The random house dictionary of the English language, the unabridged edition.* New York: Random House.

Tolman, E. C. (1932). *Purposive behavior in animals and men.* New York: Appleton-Century.

Chapter 3: The Punishment Myth

Do not hold back discipline from the child, although you strike him with the rod, he will not die.
You shall strike him with the rod, and rescue his soul from Sheol.
Psalms 23:13 and 23:14, the New American Standard Bible

It's a proven fact that capital punishment is a well-known detergent to crime.
Archie Bunker, famous fictional character from the television show "All in the Family."

What are the Real Effects of Punishment?

It's as automatic as scratching an itch, or batting a mosquito. It's as natural as growling when others do things we find irritating and hoping that they'll stop. It's as ubiquitous as a frown or a glare. We all do it--someone does something that we disapprove of, or something that upsets us, or something that we don't want them to do, or just something that drives us up the ever-lovin' wall. We want them to stop. And the first thing that crosses our minds to use in order to make the behavior stop is punishment.

Punishment and reward don't even have to be intentional—they're an intrinsic part of human interaction. Smiles and frowns, like many other facial expressions, are instinctual muscular reactions to our emotions. The positive reactions of others to our smiles and the negative reactions or others to our frowns are also instinctive. Thus, by 5 months of age, babies smile when they experience something pleasing. And when you smile encouragingly at a toddler barely old enough to walk, he or she will almost always pursue whatever behavior was currently being done with even more glee and enthusiasm. By contrast, when we frown deeply at the same child, his or her behavior becomes more hesitant and he or she may even stop entirely. The smile is reinforcing and the frown punishing, even though that may not be our deliberate intent. And as children grow, we add encouraging words, praise, hugs, food treats and gifts to our repertoire of rewards, and the children respond by doing the things we reward them for more often.

For that matter, animals also increase the frequency of a behavior when that behavior is rewarded. That's the whole basis for B. F. Skinner's operant conditioning, the most widely used and most successful animal training technique. Skinner was highly inventive in demonstrating the efficacy of rewards in making behaviors occur. He trained pigeons to play ping-pong, taught mice to dive down particular holes in a game board and avoid other holes, and even worked on the first smart weapon, a pigeon-guided bomb project pursued during WWII. Pigeons, children, your significant other, it makes no difference: reward makes the behavior that was rewarded more likely to occur in the future.

Actually, psychologists actually seldom use the word "reward," in the discussion of operant conditioning, preferring the term "reinforcement" instead. Reward is defined rather subjectively, as anything that the organism finds pleasant. Psychologists argue that a reward is something pleasing to the organism, whereas reinforcement is defined more objectively, as anything that makes an organism more likely to repeat a behavior when it's given following the occurrence of the behavior. People like Skinner didn't want to get into whether people and animals were feeling subjective pleasure, they wanted a definition that could be verified scientifically, (which, as you know after reading chapter 1, means they want a definition that can be verified empirically, by observation.) So as scientists often do, they picked a term and gave it a precise definition. In order to take advantage of that greater precision of meaning, I'll use the terms "reinforce" and "reinforcement" for the rest of this chapter rather than the more subjectively-defined "reward."

Regardless of what we call it, reinforcement makes a behavior more likely to happen again, and thus is very useful when we want a behavior to increase in frequency. What about punishment? When we consider punishment, we usually view it as the opposite of reinforcement. This makes sense on the surface, because as the punisher we're certainly taking the opposite action as we do when we were reinforcing people. Reinforcement involves bringing good things to an organism or taking away bad things, whereas punishment involves bringing bad things to an organism or taking away good things. Reinforcement makes a behavior more likely to occur in the future. Punishment is the opposite of reward. So if reward makes a behavior more likely to occur again, then punishment makes it less likely, right?

"Whoa!" You say. "Just put on the brakes there for a cotton-pickin' minute! That sounds like a set up question!" Well, you're right. And you might as well get used to set-up questions, because one pops up about every chapter. Punishment doesn't necessarily make the behavior that occurred before it less likely. What punishment does, really, is motivate us to avoid punishment in the future. One way to avoid punishment in the future is to stop the behavior that is being punished. But it's not the only way to do so. In fact, stopping the behavior isn't even the most likely outcome when we use punishment.

Let us say, for example, that 5-year-old Lutwidge picks his nose. (Here, we might as well admit that pretty much every 5-year-old is a nose picker. It seems like such a logical thing to do. Your nose is full of crinkly crud, and darned if that finger doesn't fit right up in there.) But you don't want little Lutwidge to pick his nose. For starters, once he's done so, where's the material that's now on his finger going to go? On his shirt or pants, on the dog, in his mouth--the possibilities are endless, but none of them are savory. Also, it's fairly likely that his inept little fingers with their untrimmed nails will end up scraping his nose and make it bleed. Add to those negatives that nose-picking, along with putting things in the mouth and rubbing the eyes, is one of the major vectors by which viruses are spread. Then consider the fact that no one wants to see a kid, even a cute, freckled 5-year-old, with a finger up his nose, and you've got good reason to try to break him of this habit. (In this example, and the others in this chapter, I'm using males exclusively in my examples of the effects of punishments. This is not because males are necessarily any more evil or deserving of punishment than females. Rather, I'm making a point. I use males in my examples because boys rather than girls bear the brunt of parental punishments, especially corporal punishments.)

So you decide to use punishment to stop Lutwidge's nose-picking behavior. Every time you see him picking his nose, you vow to yell at him, or spank him, or, horror of horrors, threaten to lock up his Nintendo Wii for a week. That'll stop his behavior, right? Right?

Well, did it stop you? Perhaps. Perhaps you were an easily buffaloed child, the kind of trusting, gullible kid who thought parents were omniscient and would know if you even dared to think of picking your nose. But I'm betting that you were like most children, and quickly learned that, before doing anything, you look to the left, look to the right, and look behind you. If there's no one watching, or at least no one besides your not-yet-verbal baby sister and your schnauzer, (neither of whom are going to rat you out), then you go for the nose. You didn't stop the behavior because of the punishment, you just got better at not getting caught. For the child it's the best of both worlds – he avoids punishment, but his enjoyment of the behavior can continue unabated.

It's because of this that most parents overestimate the value and the effectiveness of punishments. When they use punishments on their own children, they cease to see the behavior they're punishing. They make the rather naïve assumption that the punishment stopped the behavior, consider it another parenting job well done, and give themselves a pat on the back while smiling smugly. (You have to smile smugly when giving yourself a pat on the back or the whole effect is wasted). But the behavior hasn't been extinguished – it's just gone underground. It's one of the greatest, most widespread con jobs in the world. Children give the appearance of compliance when punishment is used by becoming very sneaky, and when questioned, by becoming very, very good liars. And because parents aren't omniscient, both of those activities, lying and being sneaky, are invariably rewarded because they help us avoid punishment most of the time. Even when lying and being sneaky doesn't enable us to avoid punishment forever, it often delays punishment. As we'll see next, for most of us, delaying punishment renders it almost as ineffective as avoiding it, at least at the moment we're doing the potentially punishable behavior.

You see, punishment, in order to be effective, must meet three criteria. It needs to be unavoidable, moderately severe, and immediate. We've already discussed the unavoidable part. If there's any way to continue a behavior and avoid a threatened punishment, that's usually what we'll do. After all, the behavior you're doing is probably being done because it's pleasurable, even if it's cheesing off your mom something fierce. If you can avoid her punishment by lying, or by concealing your actions, and still enjoy the pleasure, isn't that what you'd do?

Punishments must be moderately severe, because mild punishments just aren't going to stop any behavior that's very much fun, and very severe punishments will probably distract the child from focusing on the misbehavior to focusing just on the punishment itself. Not long ago we were discussing corporal punishment in one of my parenting classes, and one of my students pointed out that he had been the target of several quite severe spankings as a child, the kind of "go to your room and wait for me," ritualistic, and lengthy spankings that would make almost every kid's blood run cold. (But not *every* kid – we'll talk about that later.) Asked by fellow classmates if he thought the spankings had been effective in making him behave differently, my student pointed out that he didn't, in the minutes or hours or even days after each spanking, ever reconsider his behavior at all. In fact, although he remembered the spankings vividly, he couldn't recall a single example of just what he'd done to receive them. "I never thought about what I'd done," he confided to the class. "I was too busy alternately hating my dad's guts and feeling sorry for myself." Punishments that are very severe become the focus of attention rather than the behavior being punished. But punishments that are mild just aren't aversive enough to stop any behavior worth doing.

Last but not least, punishment has to be immediate. The more punishment is delayed, the lower our fear of it. The decline in fear of punishment as the punishment is delayed in time is quite a steep one. Even delaying punishment for a particular behavior by a few hours sharply diminishes the fear of the punishment. It's almost as if we think that we'll figure out how to avoid the punishment before it happens if it's down the road a bit. Meanwhile, the pleasure of the behavior that we might be punished for is immediate and strong, and if the punishment is distant enough, the potential pleasure of that immediate reward might prevail.

Consider an example of this that many people might find painfully relevant. Many people (myself included), eat way too much fat and too many carbs and exercise too little. The punishment for this constellation of behaviors is a dire one indeed – serious health problems and an early death. It's hard to think of a more severe punishment. You'd think that this threat of the ultimate punishment would drive us to eat things that are better for us and to exercise more. But the pleasure of eating and of forgoing exercise is immediate – we get it right away, this minute. The punishment is still, for most of us, years or decades down the road (at least we hope that's the case). Illness and death in 40 or 50 years is a nasty punishment, but it's too far away to motivate our behavior right now. If you knew you were going to drop dead the very next time you bit into a giant cheese burrito or a pizza or some chili fries, you'd avoid the things like a plague, and if you knew that you had to get to the gym before tonight or you were going to have a stroke, you'd be pumping iron within the hour.

But this just isn't the case – the punishment is distant, and the pleasure is now. That fact is what keeps fast food franchises doing a booming business, whereas gyms still have to institute two-for-one introductory deals and free trial offers to get customers.

For the average young child, tomorrow might as well be a month from now or even a decade away. Time passes very slowly when you're young. There are many theories as to why this is the case. One hypothesis suggests that our subjective experience of the passage of time is directly proportional to how long we've previously lived. So that when you're 5, it seems like forever until your 6th birthday, because you have to live fully one fifth of your previous whole life experience until you get to it. But if you're 50, your 51st birthday appears to come around more quickly, because it's a much shorter subjective period of time, only 1/50th of your life experience, or one-tenth the duration compared to when you were 5. The time between age 50 and 60 is, as a proportion of your life, about as long as the time you lived between ages 5 and 6. It's no wonder that months now seem to pass for me the way weeks did when we were wee tots. There are other explanations for why time seems to pass much more slowly, in general, for children than adults, as well, too many to consider in this chapter. The important issue, though, is that punishment that might not happen until the end of the week can seem like a lifetime away for small children.

Let's say Dad has baked some cookies, and quite clearly instructed you not to eat them because they're for company. He has mentioned this prohibition explicitly to you because he knows that, as a kid, you have a powerful attraction to cookies, and you have no mental concept of the idea of moderation. Also, he's put a lot of work into dinner and wants you to have a nice, healthy appetite so you'll enjoy it. Then he foolishly leaves them in easy reach and goes far enough away that you're no longer under his immediate surveillance. If you eat the cookies Dad said not to eat, you'll have a really pleasurable taste sensation right now. But if he discovers you ate the cookies, you're apt to be sent to your room for the rest of the day, or, worse yet, lose your video game privileges. Still, cookies are cookies, and they'd taste really good right now. It might be hours before he notices you ate some. Heck, he might never notice you ate some! So you might avoid the punishment entirely. And if you don't, the punishment is still hours away, and hours away is forever when you're nine. If you're like most young children, you think, "punishment, schmunishment--I like cookies!" That distant punishment just isn't that scary, not nearly scary enough to stop your behavior right now, especially if we're talking about Crisco Ultimate Chocolate Chip Cookies with bittersweet chocolate chunks. The recipe for Crisco Ultimate Chocolate Chip Cookies can be downloaded at

http://www.crisco.com/Recipes/Details.aspx?recipeID=2102

The need for punishment to be immediate is why the stereotypic refrains of punishment, "just wait until your father gets home," or "just wait until your mother gets home," are apt to be very ineffective indeed as parenting threats. Punishment that won't come until tonight is far removed from the actual behavior that is being punished, so far removed that it may not be frightening enough to stop the misbehavior at all. If it's going to be even longer until the punishment, if the child can cover up well enough that the punishment might be delayed a week or even a month, forget it.

Yet as parents, we often won't know about children's more egregious misbehaviors until long after they've occurred, and that's one of the reasons why children often are not deterred by our threats of punishment. For that matter, the same applies to adults. By the time your significant other finds out about that extravagant purchase you made (perhaps not until the credit card bill comes), you will already have been enjoying the reward of the purchase for weeks. Yes, the scene that will follow the arrival of that bill may be highly punitive, but by then the behavior has already been amply rewarded. Not only that, but the punishment will probably be only momentary, and after it occurs, you'll still be enjoying your purchase. So if another pleasurable purchase possibility comes up in the future, fear of still more distant possible punishment probably won't be enough to stop you from pulling out the card once again. This is part of the seductive evil of credit cards – I'll enjoy the purchase now, but the pain of paying for it doesn't come until later, and doesn't adequately motivate us to be thrifty right now.

Yet, despite all the evidence that punishment, at most, causes avoidance of punishment, we persist in believing that punishment makes our children's and other people's behaviors less likely. And if that wasn't enough trouble, stopping the behavior or making us figure out how to avoid the punishment aren't the only possible outcomes of punishment. Punishment also motivates the avoidance of being in the vicinity of the punisher. Let's say, for example, that your significant other comes in sweating and puffing from a jog with clothes practically dripping accumulated sweat and then sheds that clothing in the entryway or the hall and just leaves the whole sodden mess there for other people (such as you) to pick up. You're tired of this behavior (understandably) and want it to stop, so you decide to use punishment. You make a vow to scream and yell and deny the person whatever comforts you normally offer him or her (we don't need the details, thank you) until the person stops flinging foul, noisome clothing onto the carpet in the front hall and leaving it there for you to trip over when you drop in with your boss in tow for an impromptu brunch and a discussion of your long overdue promotion. Your aim is to get the person to stop the behavior, and if you yell loudly enough and the services you offer are quite spectacular, you might possibly succeed in accomplishing that goal. In this case, it's not like your significant other can simply avoid the punishment by lying or concealing his or her actions, because there's no hiding that the saturated mass that was his or her jogging suit is lying on the floor, and thus there is no way to avoid getting caught. But you have to consider another possibility—your significant other may choose to avoid punishment by avoiding the punisher. That is, he or she may decide that you're not worth the trouble, dump you, and take up with someone who doesn't punish this particular behavior.

If you genuinely care for the person and were anticipating a bright future together involving a cat, a dog, a picket fence, and the pitty-pitty-patter of little-bitty feet, this isn't the outcome you're going for. Yet inspiring others to avoid you is a genuine possibility when you use punishment on them, especially if you use it frequently. I met a fellow once whose son, the minute he turned 18, ran out and got a nose ring. We're not talking about a subtle, tasteful little hoop of 18k gold here, we're talking about a ring made of black iron that would make your average bull proud (and possibly a bit droopy-nosed). The father absolutely hated the ring in his son's nose from the moment he first caught sight of it. So he decided, perhaps not even consciously, that he'd make his son get rid of the ring by punishing him for having it. He began ridiculing the kid every time he saw him wearing the ring, assuming that his ridicule would make his son quit wearing the ring. What the son did instead was simply stop coming over when he knew his father was home, shifting his schedule to visit his mother in the afternoons instead. Pretty soon the fellow was wondering why he never saw his son any more, not realizing that this common outcome was a direct result of his using punishment.

Social psychologist John Gotman, emeritus at the University of Washington, has spent years investigating the quality of relationships between couples, between relatives, and between friends. He's proposed an interesting idea that goes by the popular name of the "Five to One Rule" (Gottman, 2003). It's a very simple idea, really. He and his colleagues have observed that in relationships, if you document how many positive interactions the pair have and compare the number of those interactions with the number of negative interactions they have, you can predict how long the relationship will last and whether it appears to be in trouble. Ratios higher than five positive encounters for every negative experience are associated with relationships that are strong and long-lasting. Relationships with fewer than five positive encounters for every negative one are more likely to be in trouble or even doomed to failure. Punishments are negative encounters, so the more they're used rather than rewards, the more danger the relationship is in, proportionally speaking. Under the Five to One Rule, you'd need five positive interactions in the relationship to balance up every usage of punishment. If that doesn't happen, the relationship would quickly sour. But that just supports the risk of punishment we looked at in the previous paragraph, the risk that punishment will motivate the person to avoid the punisher.

The next issue you have to consider, when you contemplate using punishment, is whether the punishment will have any effect on the behavior at all. Most behaviors that we want to eradicate in other people are occurring because they're rewarding. Some of those behaviors are very, very rewarding, and that category includes a lot of the things we'd like to keep teenagers from doing, such as drinking alcohol, using drugs, and engaging in sexual behavior. To stop such behaviors, a punishment has to be more aversive than the behavior is rewarding. But in the case those three behaviors, it's had to find a punishment severe enough to fit that criterion that doesn't involve half-killing the person. Any punishment that is less aversive than the behavior is rewarding, will simply be accepted as part of the price of getting the reward.

For example, almost all kids have a curfew of some sort or another in adolescence. Yet pretty much all of them, at one point or another, find themselves at a party or gathering so stimulating and enticing that they catch themselves looking at their watches and making this calculation-- "Okay, how much fun am I having, and how much trouble will I be in if I don't go home now?" And if the party is really fun, a regular lollapalooza of a party (at least in your limited 16-year-old scale of experience), odds are pretty good that the curfew is going to be violated, with whatever punishment that is coming down the road being considered just the cost of a good time.

It's one of the reasons why people will continue to use drugs even when they're looking some very severe penalties right in the face. Think of how many times we've heard the stories of movie and television personalities who are on probation for drug use, who have been told right up front by a stern, frowning judge that they were going back to jail if they are ever even so much as in the same zip code as an illegal drug, who nonetheless in short order were caught stoned out of their gourds? The punishment was very, very severe, and the risk of punishment was significant. But the pleasure of the drugs was apparently well worth the risk.

Punishments also may have no effect at all on some behaviors. This is because humans, and animals too, have a tremendous ability to adapt to just about any level of suffering if they experience it long enough. If we're exposed to enough punishment for a long enough period of time, we habituate to it. We get used to that level of suffering, it becomes the norm, and we learn to live with it. Alan Parducci, emeritus of the University of California,

Los Angeles, explained this in his Contextual Theory of Happiness (Parducci, 1968). Parducci argued that we judge how happy or unhappy we are by comparing what we're going through now with what we've experienced in the recent past. If things are going much better right now than we remember them going before, we get downright giddy. If things are going much worse than we remember them being before, we feel unhappy and depressed. So if you win the lottery, you feel great right afterward because what just happened is much better than what you've been going through up to then. For awhile you're walking on air. But a few weeks later you may very well be unhappy, because you quickly adjust to a more lavish lifestyle, and in comparison to the day you won the lottery, things aren't really all that great now.

Reactions to punishment are very similar. If you seldom experience unpleasantness, but due to punishment things are unpleasant now, you will find that unpleasantness very aversive and you may be highly motivated to end it, possibly even by behaving yourself. But if your life is always unpleasant, a little unpleasantness right now in the form of punishment is just more of the same, something to be expected, and unlikely to motivate you to change things.

So let's say you're a parent who relies on punishment a lot. Twelve-year-old Lutwidge does something you don't approve of, so you ground him for a week. By the end of the week, he's done something else, so you ground him awhile longer. He gets off being grounded for a day, and then he's done something else and you ground him again. Do this enough, and when you say, "you're grounded," Lutwidge will say to himself, "big deal, I'm always grounded." And it's true. Grounding is his usual state. He's learned to live life while grounded. He's learned how to use email and instant messages, how to use Twitter and Facebook and how to maintain a social life on a cell phone. He's learned to schedule social events before coming home, and he's learned how to disguise social visits as class projects and study sessions and library visits. He may even have learned how to sneak out his bedroom window in the middle of the night and climb down a drainpipe, a trellis, or a tree (or just leap out of his window onto the ground if you guys have a typical one-story ranch like the one I call home). He's habituated to the punishment, and it's no longer all that aversive. A new grounding isn't any different from what he's used to in the recent past, so he's not all that unhappy. Because of hedonic contrast combined with excessive reliance on punishment, grounding ceases to be punitive, and becomes nothing but the status quo.

Now consider the child who's never been grounded, a child who's used to having an evening social life, coming and going as he pleases, and so on. Tell him he's grounded and he'll be devastated. It's a big change from what he's used to in the immediate past, so he's very unhappy and finds the punishment very aversive. But it's only that aversive because he so rarely has experienced it. If he'd been punished that way a lot (as is the case with poor Lutwidge), it would stop being as aversive.

There's an irony here, because it means that punishment is most effective when it's used the least. The more it's used, the more the person adjusts to it and the less aversive it is. Kids who are hardly punished at all are strongly affected by threats of punishments, but those who are punished frequently aren't deterred at all by punishment threats. This is true even of the most intense and aversive punishments. We all know parents who are screamers, who berate children verbally for every little thing they do. Invariably, those children become extremely good at ignoring parental disapproval as well as loud noises. Mom's mad, but Mom's always mad. Why is today different from any other day, and why should I worry about it?

Then there are the times when punishment actually increases the frequency of behavior. This usually happens when the person being punished is bored and receiving very little attention. Punishment, by its nature, almost always brings attention along with it during the punishment. And after the punishment, the punisher is apt to feel a bit guilty (or more than a bit guilty if the punishment is severe), and thus he or she may actually be more supportive, rewarding, and solicitous than normal. The attention gained by earning punishment and the positive interactions that follow the punishment, when all has been forgiven, may be well worth suffering the punishment itself, especially when punishments aren't all that severe.

Here's a case in point. Every grade school class has its attention pig – the kid who craves attention so badly that he or she will do anything to get it, including things that result in punishment. Whenever class gets too boring, or the work gets too hard, these kids act out. Acting out gets them punished, getting punished always involves getting attention, and if that weren't enough, the teacher often feels a bit sorry for the child after punishing him and may treat him a bit more positively for a period afterward out of guilt. So the punishment is actually rewarding, on the balance, and when behaviors (or misbehaviors, in this case) are rewarded, they increase in frequency. The net result is that, instead of reducing the attention pig's misbehavior, the teacher actually ends up increasing it.

So after considering all these complex effects of punishments, where do we end up? The bottom line is this: punishments are often only of limited effectiveness, and generally aren't nearly as effective as most parents or teachers think. Punishment is our first impulse whenever other people irritate us, but punishment is usually not our best choice as a tool of discipline because it's so unpredictable in its effects. Punishment may stop a behavior, but it's more likely to teach the person how to avoid punishment instead by avoiding getting caught or avoiding the punisher. Punishment, when used often, causes the punished person to habituate to it, adjusting until the punishment ceases to be anything but the norm and is no longer aversive. Punishment may also have no effect on the behavior if the reward of the behavior is more pleasurable than the punishment is aversive. Punishment may actually increase the behavior if the punishment brings attention and attention is something the person craves. What I'm saying here, is that punishment involves one of the most egregious cases of undeserved positive press in existence. It seldom does what it purports to do and what most people believe it does, yet it maintains the façade of doing so in almost everyone's minds.

The People Punishment Never Works On, or Why One Size Doesn't Fit All

Still, despite all these complications, some people are adamant supporters of punishment, including punishments of the body, or corporal punishments. I've met any number of people, most of them men rather than women, who challenge my argument that punishment seldom stops people from doing punished behaviors. Consider this post, one of many that circulate round and round on Facebook:

Have to laugh at people who are against spanking.. My parents whipped my booty like there was no tomorrow... I didn't hate them... I didn't have trust issues with them because of it... I didn't fear them... But I sure respected them! And I learned what my boundaries were, and knew what would happen it If broke them!
Re-post if you got your tail tore up and survived it!
(Copied from a Facebook post, August, 2011)

So is spanking, or punishment in general, a necessary part of child rearing, so necessary that, like the many people who've reposted the above statement suggest, we have to laugh at people who are against it? We've already talked about how some people overestimate the effectiveness of punishments in general and corporal punishments in particular because they don't realize that the behavior they're punishing has simply gone underground. But we're not talking about that here—these are people who were punished for violating limits that had been set by their parents, and they as children ceased the behavior that was punished, sooner or later. Of course, they could still be mistaken about causation here, because we're talking about correlational data. It's possible that, rather than the punishment having stopped their misbehavior, their misbehavior stopped because they didn't want to upset their parents, or because they had learned to control their impulses as they grew older, or simply because they finally learned the rules their parents had set for them.

But even if it is true that punishment alone is what made these Facebook reposters eventually learn to behave themselves, they're still making a giant and probably false assumption. They're assuming that because a particular punishment like spanking worked on them, that same punishment will work on every child. To see why this is a false assumption, we'll have to detour for a moment and consider why people, in general, learn to behave morally and avoid immoral behavior.

Martin Hoffman (Hoffman, 1988) has argued that there are three reasons people behavior morally. They are (in no particular order)

1. Anticipation of immediate or future rewards or punishments
2. Empathy for others
3. Logical reasoning

These three factors, what I like to call the "tripod of morality," are all pretty self-explanatory. As we've already discussed, anticipation of reward and punishment hinges on being observed by others while engaged in good or bad behavior, and thus is less powerful in situations where others aren't going to know what we're doing. Empathy refers to the fact that we feel the emotions of others, so we share other people's happiness and suffer other people's pain. Thus, if we were to help other people, we'll benefit from their pleasure, and if we were to hurt other people, we'll suffer, too. Logical reasoning also is important—there are good, logical reasons to behave well and to avoid bad behavior, and we understand those reasons more completely as we get older and our reasoning abilities improve.

When it comes to anticipation and fear of punishment, including fear of painful physical punishments, we're not all created equal. Some people have more tolerance for suffering and pain than others when physical punishments actually occur. Also, when it comes to advance fear of punishments, some people just aren't very emotionally reactive. For a variety of reasons both biological and environmental, there are people whose emotional systems doesn't get worked up over much of anything. They don't show advance fear of punishments because they have such low levels of emotional reaction that fear of punishment isn't aversive – it may even be mildly exciting. (Such children may show actual fear of punishment while it is happening, but it's advance fear of punishment that deters us from misbehavior—reaction to punishment after the behavior has occurred has no deterrence value at all.)

People with low emotional reactions generally have a deficit involving a second leg of the tripod of morality as well. In addition to not fearing punishment, they don't feel much empathy for others. Thus, they don't feel bad when they cause other people to suffer harm. Such folks are often left with anticipation of reward and logical reasoning as their only motivations for being good. Psychologists have a diagnostic category for these people who have such low overall emotional arousal potential that they don't fear punishment and don't care if they hurt others. We call them antisocial personalities.

Antisocial personality is traceable to a wide variety of causal factors, which together result in the person having a very low level of emotional arousal. They might have been born with the potential for normal levels of emotional arousal but suffered through such horrible conditions as children that they learned to block those emotions or simply stopped feeling them. Or they might have been born with very low potential for arousal to start with because of genetic or biological conditions or both, and nothing in their environments raised that ability during childhood. Generally, combinations of both of these general factors are involved.

However it came to be, this low emotional arousal potential makes these individuals different from other children and adults. When the rest of us hurt other people, empathy makes us feel their pain and suffering, pain and suffering caused by our actions, and that means we're getting punished for or misbehavior. We also have normal emotional arousal to advance threats of punishments, arousal aversive enough that we are frightened of the prospect of punishment and adjust our behavior to avoid it. But antisocial personalities have such low emotional arousal levels that they don't feel empathy, and they don't have advance fear of punishment either. If they don't develop other reasons to behave morally, that's a very bad combination indeed.

Now, technically, psychologists don't apply the term "antisocial personality" to people under 18. Instead, people who are under 18 who have very low emotional arousal and little empathy or advance fear of punishment are said to have "conduct disorder." Conduct disorder is basically junior antisocial personality. But the committees that authored the big book of mental illnesses published by the American Psychiatric Association, currently the Diagnostic and Statistical Manual-IV-TR, but soon to be replaced by the DSM-V, didn't want to brand a child with a pejorative label like "antisocial personality," so they invented a different term to apply to children with the similar symptoms.

Antisocial personality and childhood conduct disorder are strongly connected. When you run across an adult with antisocial personality, that person has shown a marked lack of empathy and no fear of punishment for many years, generally all the way back into childhood. The same people who were setting cats on fire when they were ten are getting pleasure torturing people when they're twenty. The same people who don't mind lying, cheating, and stealing as adults also didn't mind lying, cheating, and stealing as children. It's not that such people are doomed from childhood onward – with the right experiences, some children with conduct disorder grow out of it. They're also not doomed to remain like that for life. Many people who have antisocial personality may also develop more of an aversion to punishment as they get older, often after the age of 30 or 35—it's one of the reason why many life-long criminals go straight from mid-life onward. But until that point, we've got this group of people who don't respond normally to threats of punishment and don't feel empathy for others, and they're quite a handful.

There is evidence that genes play a role in this condition, and thus that genes may predispose some people to more easily become law-breakers. One of the most widely cited studies in the psychology of criminal behavior is the famous "Danish Adoption Study." Denmark has completely open adoption records, which makes it possible for researchers to do all sorts of studies of how similar adopted children are to their biological parents as well as to their adoptive parents. The people who did the Danish Adoption study split children who had been adopted into two groups, those whose biological parents had committed registered criminal offenses, and those who had not. Then they took those two groups and split them each into two additional groups, those who had adoptive parents who committed registered criminal offenses, and those who had not. Thus, they ended up with four groups: children whose adoptive and biological parents both were criminals, children whose adoptive parents were criminals but their biological parents were not, children whose biological parents were criminals but their adoptive parents were not, and children whose adoptive parents were not criminals and neither were their biological parents.

When the adopted children had neither biological nor adoptive parents who committed registered criminal offenses, 10.5% of them had committed registered criminal offenses themselves. When they had biological parents who had not committed any offenses but adopted parents who had, it was found that 11.5% of them had committed criminal offenses, essentially the same number as the previous group with no criminal parents. But when the adopted children's biological parents had committed registered criminal offenses but not the adoptive parents, the children's rate of criminal offenses climbed to 22%. And when both biological and adoptive parents committed registered criminal offenses, the percentage of child offenders climbed even more, to 36.2%, or more than a third of the population! (Hutchings and Mednick, 1977)

What does all this data suggest? It suggests a genetic propensity or a group of propensities that make criminal behavior somewhat more likely is being passed from biological parents to their children. The criminal behavior of adoptive parents, does not, by itself, make adoptive children more likely to engage in criminal behavior. But having a biological parent who committed criminal acts doubles the rate of criminal behavior, even though those criminal parents themselves did not raise the children. That doesn't mean environment doesn't matter, though, because when the children had both the biological tendency from criminal biological parents and the role model of criminal adoptive parents, odds of criminal behavior by the child more than tripled compared to children with no criminal parents of any kind.

Very low emotional arousal is a good candidate for one of those genetic propensities that make criminal behavior more likely. Threats of punishments frighten normal people and make them avoid behavior that might lead to such punishments. Empathy for others drives us to avoid doing bad things to other people and to do good things for them instead. It's easy to assume that punishments and empathy have that same effect on everyone else that they do on us. But neither children with conduct disorder nor adults with antisocial personality fear punishments much, if at all, and they don't feel empathy, either. They don't even think about punishments until the punishments are being carried out, and by then it's too late to have much in the way of deterrent value (or detergent value, if you're Archie Bunker).

Let me illustrate this with an example from my own experience. Many years ago, I knew a very nice couple who were temporarily taking care of a distant relative, an 11-year-old boy with a history of poor behavior. He showed no empathy for the feelings of animals or people – for example, if you didn't watch him he'd be poking animals with a cattle prod or a sharp stick for no particular reason, or casually stealing or breaking some other kid's possessions. The foster parents grounded him, took away his video games and toys, gave him extra chores to do, and generally threatened him with an escalating series of punishments trying to get him to stop all the antisocial behavior. They had him meet with religious figures who warned him of the spiritual dangers of his behavior. Finally, at wit's end, they told him that if he didn't stop getting in trouble at school they were going to give him the spanking of his life. That had such deterrent value that the very next day, at school, he destroyed an antique wooden box that a fellow student had brought in as part of a cultural unit in history class. As they were leaving the classroom for lunch, he simply reached out and knocked the valuable, irreplaceable family heirloom off the teacher's desk, then jumped on it with both feet. The teacher raged, the principal raged, and when the foster parents were called, they raged, too. They asked him why he did it, and he just shrugged and said, "I don't know." They asked him if he didn't feel sorry for the girl whose family treasure he destroyed, and he just shrugged again. They reminded him that they'd promised him the worst spanking of his life if he misbehaved again, and he just shrugged some more.

Like the parents described in the Facebook blurb I cited earlier, these parents determined to get through to their little miscreant through the spanking they'd promised him. Once they got home, his foster father picked him up around the waist, tucked him under one arm (he was a smallish kid) and lugged him down to the basement, where he proceeded to give him the kind of spanking that would have given most children nightmares thereafter, and had them becoming models of stellar behavior until they were 36, at the very least. "Now maybe he'll know I mean business," he reported thinking to himself. Finally, deciding the kid had had enough, or maybe just unable to go on himself (he had normal levels of empathy, after all, and found hurting a child very unpleasant), he stopped the punishment and set the boy on his feet. According to his later report, the boy pulled up his pants swiftly with his head bowed, then covered his face with both hands, breathing hard, and stood there for a long moment. "I'm sorry I had to do that," he remembered saying. The boy was shaking, and making little snorting noises. Feeling guilty already, the foster father reached to pull the boy close, to hug him and tell him that he still loved him and that the spanking was necessary in order to guide him into being a better, more moral person. And that's when he realized the boy's shaking and snorting wasn't crying. He was laughing—laughing uncontrollably. "It was the most cold-blooded thing I've ever seen," he told me later. "I asked him if he wanted another spanking, and he just laughed harder. What do you do with a kid like that?"

Well, you don't threaten him with even more punishment, that's obvious. If that level of punishment isn't working, you're obviously barking up the wrong tree, and the raccoon you were tracking is scampering across the treetops in the other direction. Threats of punishment might work on those of us with normal levels of emotional arousal, and might work superbly on those who are very emotional. But such threats just aren't that scary for people who have very low levels of arousal, and who don't get worked up about much of anything. Neither does imploring them to think how bad they've made other people feel. The usual methods parents rely on most heavily to make kids behave just aren't that effective with people with low emotional arousal, people who are possible candidates to have conduct disorder or to be antisocial personalities. Parents often respond to this lack of success by making the punishments more severe, but it often takes unimaginable levels of punishment to get a rise out of most people with antisocial personality, and it may not work even then, as in the example above.

So do threats of punishment deter bad behavior by children, and more serious and violent crime by adults? Yes and no. For most of us, the answer is a clear "yes." You'd be petrified at the possibility of spending even a month in the overcrowded hellholes that constitute most American maximum security prisons, let alone years or an entire lifetime. The fact that you might be injured or killed would make you avoid fights or confrontations, and the possibility of receiving the death penalty would keep you from attempting to kill another even if you hated that person with your very heart and soul. We prescribe draconian punishments for behaviors we abhor, and assume that the horrendous nature of those punishments will stop those behaviors, because such threats work on us. If the behaviors then continue, and most of them do, our response is to make the punishments even more harsh, assuming that "getting tough on crime" is the solution to preventing it. But people with very low emotional arousal aren't deterred by the threat of even very severe punishments. A prime example of this is the fruit of the "War on Drugs."

The official "War on Drugs" began in the Nixon administration in 1969. The name itself was inspired by Lyndon Johnson's "War on Poverty," an initiative of the previous administration that was about equally successful in eradicating poverty as the war on drugs has turned out to be in eradicating that scourge. The amount of money the United States Federal Government and state governments have spent in interception operations, drug task forces, incarceration, prosecution, and conviction of drugs users and sellers, and the amount spent in policing operations in the 40 years is absolutely astonishing, recently running to about 60 billion dollars a year. Millions of people have been jailed for drug use and drug sales in that time. The penalties for drug sales, especially, have increased dramatically over the years, until now you can get life in prison without parole for some sales offenses. Life in prison is a pretty aversive punishment. So how's that old war on drugs been going?

You know the answer to that one. Illegal drugs are readily available in every part of the United States, despite the harsh penalties for sales and for use. The prisons are bursting with people imprisoned on drug offenses, yet drugs are as readily available as before. What's going on here?

Part of the problem is that the people who use drugs often become the people who sell them as well. And the people who use drugs are often people with low levels of emotional arousal, perhaps even verging on the levels experienced by antisocial personalities. Nothing much excites these people, not the usual joys or triumphs, not the pleasures that most of us enjoy. They're attracted to drugs in part because only drugs make them feel the pleasure that most people enjoy frequently just from living life. And they don't fear punishment for using drugs because of that same low level of arousal. Tell them that they'll face serious penalties if they're caught selling drugs, they just shrug, the way the boy in my above example shrugged when threatened with a spanking – it doesn't excite them, it doesn't scare them, and it certainly doesn't make them stop selling drugs. Yes, life in prison would deter <u>you</u> from selling drugs, but you aren't selling drugs anyway. (At least most of you aren't. Those of you who are really ought to cut it out, because it ticks off the rest of us something awful.)

Contrary to the belief of the Facebook posters and others who defend corporal punishment, the sad truth is that the majority of juvenile delinquents and violent teens, far from being coddled by permissive parents, tend to have parents who use corporal punishments frequently. In the words of Dr. Ralph Welsh, who as a doctor for a juvenile facility has given psychological exams to over 2,000 delinquents,

"I have yet to see a repeat male delinquent that wasn't raised on a belt, board, cord, or fist…it is now apparent that the recidivist male delinquent who was never struck with a belt, board, extension cord, fist, or an equivalent is virtually nonexistent… As the severity of corporal punishment in the delinquent's developmental history

increases, so does the probability that he will engage in a violent act." (Email from Dr. Ralph Welsh to the Dallas School District in response to a decision to use of the paddle in Dallas schools.)

Many of these repeat juvenile defenders are people with very low emotional arousal levels. As young children, when they didn't respond to mild punishments, their parents reacted by escalating the punishments, and when this still didn't bring good behavior, they escalated the punishments again, some continuing the pattern until it became seriously abusive. And still these children had behavior problems, because they don't experience sufficient fear of the punishments to come, at least not enough to prevent them from doing impulsive, ill advised things.

This is why the "one size fits all" discipline techniques don't work on such children. Threats of spanking or other punishments may indeed strike powerful fear into most children. Yet those are also the children who are most likely to behave themselves anyway through the use of other techniques such as rewards, empathy for others, reasoning, and logical persuasion. Substantial evidence exists that people of very low emotional arousal, people who are at risk of having childhood conduct disorder and adult antisocial personality, will respond to tangible rewards, such as money and prizes, and that they're just as responsive to reasoning as everyone else. Parents have to recognize the need to shift tactics with such children. Our first impulse is almost always to punish, but we should usually go with our second or third impulse instead.

Logical and Natural Punishments

Even knowing the limits of punishments, we all use them, because there are times that punishments work, and because punishment is everyone's first reaction to every irritating behavior. Even the most enlightened parent is going to use punishment on children, and the most enlightened adults also use punishment on each other. You're a human, and that means you're going to punish people. So it's important to understand that not all punishments are equal. Some punishments are easier to use and more effective than others. Surprisingly, it's not a matter of how harsh or aversive the punishments are, either. What it really all boils down to how arbitrary and artificial the punishments are.

Let's say that you get in your car in the driveway, start the engine, and start to back up. Just in the nick of time, you see the edge of a handlebar in your mirror and slam on the brakes only moments before backing over your child's bicycle. Once again, little Lutwidge has jumped off of it and left it lying in the driveway, in danger of being backed over or stolen.

Most Americans would immediately feel that punishment is in order here. Some parents might, in fact, rush into the house and immediately corner the miscreant and administer a sound spanking, or yank the plug out on his Nintendo Wii midgame and pronounce that playing games is off limits for two weeks because the bike was left in the driveway. Either punishment is bound to be aversive for normal children. You're hoping Lutwidge will stop leaving the bike in the driveway in order to avoid whichever punishment you used. He certainly can't avoid the punishment in this case, because you'll always know when he left the bike in the driveway, so what's the problem?

The problem is that both of the punishments mentioned above are screamingly arbitrary. There's no logical connection between being unable to play video games and leaving the bike in the driveway, or between pain in the child's posterior and leaving the bike in the driveway. You say to the child, "Well, I had to do that because of your misbehavior," but that makes no sense at all, and any child over the age of 3 knows it doesn't make any sense. You didn't have to administer that particular punishment all—you simply chose to because such punishments come readily to mind and are easy to administer. Yet neither punishment has any logical connection to the child's misbehavior.

"But that's just the way punishments are," you protest. (It's amazing that I can hear your protests so well clear over here in California.) Well, consider this. Suppose that rather than storming into the house and seizing the Wii, (a device totally innocent of the child's misbehavior), you take the bicycle that you found behind the car and wheel it to the garage, where you chain it to the wall and then lock the chain. When Lutwidge eventually discovers his bike chained and unusable in the garage and comes to ask about it, you calmly explain that you found it behind the car where it was in danger of being crushed or stolen, and in order to make sure it would remain safe you chained it securely in the garage. When he or she protests, "But I want to ride it," you calmly explain that the bike was in danger and you had to take steps to keep it safe by locking it up. You then mention that the bike will be unchained in a week or two. When it is, you trust that the bike will not be left in an inappropriate location again. If so, it will have to be chained up longer for both its own safety and the sake of your car.

This is also a punishment – you're taking a good thing away from the child. But it's a logical punishment. The problem is that the bike was in jeopardy, and it won't be in jeopardy if it's chained in the garage. Taking away the child's Wii won't make the bike any safer, and neither will smacking his hindquarters, but simply locking it up is a punishment that also goes right to the root of the problem – it's a logical punishment.

Some logical punishments are also natural punishments. A natural punishment is the natural consequence of an act, the thing that would normally happen if a particular act is committed. For example, as Tevye points out in *Fiddler on the Roof*, "if you spit in the air, it lands in your face." Having spit land on your face is the natural consequence of spitting in the air – it happens every time you do the behavior, and, assuming that you find spit landing on your face to be aversive, you'll probably quickly learn to avoid spitting in the air.

Sometimes allowing the natural consequences of a behavior ensue is the best way to punish a behavior. When I had children in grade school, the school once sent out a parent memo announcing that they would no longer accept school lunches, homework, jackets, or other items that children had forgotten. Having had children of my own, I can attest that anything that isn't attached to them permanently will be left behind at home at one point or another, usually repeatedly. When a school has hundreds of students, the number of parents dropping things by on a given day becomes enormous, hence the school's refusal to accept any more such items.

This is a good example of a situation where the natural consequences of a behavior might be the most effective course for most parents, anyway. What is the natural consequence if you yourself forget your lunch? You have to go hungry, or beg food from other people, or come up with your own hard-earned cash to buy food. What happens if you forget your coat? You get chilly, and getting chilly is a natural consequence of forgetting your coat. What happens if you forget your homework? You get lower grades, you have to do makeup work, you have to do extra credit, or you end up in summer school, all of which are the natural consequences of not turning in homework. You don't have to invent punishments in these situations – the situation is naturally punitive, and the punishment is unavoidable – unless, that is, you have indulgent parents who rush in with your lunch, jacket, or homework every time you forget it.

Natural punishments aren't always ideal. They can create problems for the parent and might involve an unconscionable waste of funds and resources. The natural consequences of leaving your bike behind the car would be that the bike is run over. But this would be a terrible waste of a perfectly good bicycle and the resources and effort taken to produce that bicycle, and permanent deprivation of it would probably be a much more severe punishment than the behavior calls for (not to mention the fact that it's your hard-earned cash that probably paid for the bike to start with). Likewise, if your child becomes unable to get into college because he doesn't turn in homework, it's you he is going to come back to and sponge off of when he can't make a living. In such cases, a logical consequence such as mandatory extra credit homework to make up for the missing assignments is preferable to the natural consequence.

Misbehavior can also be dealt with by other means besides either rewards or punishments. Sometimes a parent can alter a child's behavior just by making compliance easier. A while back I had a social visit at the home of a young mother who mentioned that her two little boys, aged 5 and 7, were continually disobeying her concerning the proper treatment of dirty clothing. She said that they refused to put their dirty clothes in the hamper, despite the fact that she'd yelled at them, taken away their favorite toys, and banned their TV time as punishments. She pointed to the bathroom in the hall, saying, "They just heave their clothes on the floor next to the bathtub, and then they leave them there! Look, there's a dirty shirt there now!" She then stalked into the bathroom and scooped up the shirt, then walked past me down the hall, through the house, out to the utility porch, and tossed the offending shirt into a hamper by the washer. It turns out that it was this hamper that she expected the children to use.   In other words, she wanted the kids to take their clothes off and bathe, then pick the clothes up and walk the entire length of the house to put them in a hamper before scampering off to bed.

I asked her if she'd considered putting a hamper in the bathroom, and she said there wasn't room, and besides, she couldn't find one that matched the décor. I finally persuaded her to put a hamper in the boys' room nearby. I week later I bumped into her and she was all smiles. "You're a genius," she said. "I haven't had to pick up a thing all week!"

Sadly, I'm not a genius, I don't even play one on TV. I just was far enough from the problem to see what she didn't see, that sometimes we make it unnecessarily difficult for people to comply with our wishes without realizing it.   If you want kids to use tissues for their runny noses, put them within easy reach of where kids are – next to the computer, the video game, the TV, their work desks, and their beds. They're far more likely to use them if they're handy and not clear across the house somewhere. If you want your kids to stay on task when they do homework, set up a homework area where distractions are minimal.

Don't forget, too, that children respond to reasoning, even at very young ages (we are Homo Sapiens, after all, "men of wisdom." We're Homo Sapiens from the moment we're born. Children may be ignorant of many things, but they're not stupid). Give people, including children, good, logical reasons why they should do what we want them to do. The advantage of reasoning over punishments is that reasoning works even when we're not around, even in cases where the child might otherwise get away with misbehavior. If you can't think of a good logical reason for the child to do what you want him or her to do, you have to ask yourself why is it that you want him or her to do it in the first place?

Children are also more likely to follow the rules if you give them a say in the making of the rules themselves. We all are more likely to follow a plan we helped produce and thus can see the reasons for and understand. So sit down and work things out with your children. State the problem that prompted the meeting, ask the child for suggestions in addressing the problem, make some suggestions of your own, and get an agreement on how the problem will be addressed and a commitment to follow that solution. As is the case with adults, children prefer to have a say in their lives, and they're more likely to follow rules that they supported.

Punishments are often our first impulse when people displease us. Yet, we should often go with our second, or third, or even fourth impulse. As the old saying goes, you catch a lot more flies with honey than vinegar. We should consider rewarding the behavior we want rather than punishing the behavior we don't, we should provide people with explanations for why we want the behavior to stop, we should make compliance as easy as we can whenever possible, and we should teach people what behaviors to do instead of the behavior we're punishing. And when we do use punishments, our punishments should be natural or logical punishments.

But most important, our punishments should be sparing. Punishments work best when they're hardly used at all. Not only does this make meeting the five to one ratio of good to bad encounters more likely, ensuring continuing good relations with our children and other associates, but punishments become more aversive the less they're used, and less aversive the more they're used. When you add to it that heavy use of punishment encourages deceit to avoid punishment, and that punishments often don't work at all on the world's least well-behaved people, the true picture of the punishment myth becomes clear.

References:

Gottman, J. (2003). *The Mathematics of Marriage*. Boston: MIT Press.

Hoffman, M. L. (1988) Moral development. In M. H. Bornsteing and M. E. Lamb (Eds.) *Developmental psychology: An advanced textbook.* Hillsdale, NJ: Erlbaum.

Hutchings, B., & Mednick, S. A. (1977). Criminality in adoptees and their adoptive and biological parents: A pilot study. In S. A. Mednick and K. O. Christiansen (Eds.), *Biosocial bases of criminal behavior* (p. 127-141). New York: Gardner Press.

New American Standard Bible. (1971). Anaheim, CA: Foundation Publications.

Parducci, Allen (1968). The Relativism of Absolute Judgment. *Scientific American, 219*, 84-90.

Recipe for Ultimate Chocolate Chip Cookies. Retrieved from http://www.crisco.com/Recipes/Details.aspx?recipeID=2102

Welsh, Ralph (2003) Research does not lie. Retrieved from http://www.nospank.net/welsh9.htm

Dr. Dean Richards

Chapter 4: Mental Illness by Committee

"I do not have ADD—ooh, shiny thing!" Comedian Bill Engvall

Attention deficit hyperactivity disorder and reading disorder (dyslexia) have a number of things in common. Both occur in childhood, and both disrupt school performance. The two also sometimes coincide, in that it's not uncommon for people with attention deficit disorder to have reading disorder as well. Attention deficit hyperactivity disorder is diagnosed when an individual has an extreme inability to focus attention. People with ADHD have a much greater than normal number of problems compared to other people their age in staying on task, resisting distractions, controlling impulses, and doing what they're supposed to do and avoiding doing what they're not supposed to do. They have a terrible time in school and troubles at work as well when they're older, and they tend to be viewed by others as being irritating, irresponsible, undisciplined, and often just plain difficult. In a 2002 study, the Mayo Clinic reported ADHD diagnoses as being quite common, striking about 7.5% of the American children. (Mayo Clinic, 2002) (The number really should be 5%, but more about that later.)

Reading disorder (no longer called "dyslexia" by psychologists and psychiatrists for reasons we'll detail below) involves having reading achievement that is substantially below that expected of a person of that age, and also far below the person's intellectual abilities. This deficit is also not due to any sensory difficulties the person might have. In addition, this low reading achievement level also must interfere substantially with ability to function in society. Reading disorder rates in the United States have been estimated at between 5% and 17% of the population.

These two common childhood learning disorders have a couple of less well-known commonalities. The first is that both are conditions that occur primarily because of problems the individual has in fitting into his or her environment, not because of something inherently wrong with the individual him or herself. In different environments both currently and in the past, people with each of these conditions were not seen as being as problematic as they are in this particular society at this particular time. The second thing these two disorders have in common is that both of them have no clear-cut line where presence of the disorder ends and normalcy begins.

Attention Deficit Hyperactivity Disorder

To understand why a particular human condition might be a problem in some environments and not others, and why it's not always clear who has a disorder and who doesn't, we have to look at the process of how mental illness diagnoses are arrived at in general, and how diagnoses of ADHD and reading disorder are arrived at specifically. Who decides what mental illnesses we acknowledge, who decides who has those mental illnesses, and how do they make that decision?

The model of diagnosis used for mental illnesses closely mirrors the model of diagnosis used for physical illnesses. First, we try to identify symptoms: ways that people with the illness differ from those who lack the illness. Those symptoms are then grouped together into syndromes, groups of symptoms that tend to happen simultaneously. That group of symptoms is then given a name. If your lungs are filling with fluid and are becoming inflamed, and you're having trouble breathing to the extent it's causing you great concern, you probably have pneumonia. If you're running a fever and have broken out in a spotty rash all over your body, you probably have chicken pox. If you're hearing voices when no one is around, and have delusions of grandeur and persecution, and are not making sense when you talk, you probably have schizophrenia. If you like to loot companies of all their equity and then bail out on a golden parachute taking a big chunk of the remaining company assets with you, you're probably a corporate raider.

Okay, that last one isn't a recognized syndrome, (but perhaps it ought to be). Anyway, once we have identified a syndrome and given it a name, we can talk about the syndrome using that name, simplifying our conversations about it, and ensuring everyone knows what set of symptoms we're discussing. This is especially important for medical recording purposes, research purposes, and for the purposes of billing when we're talking about Medicare or health insurance coverage. We also can then start looking for the cause or causes of our syndrome, and, if we find them, we can add them to the list of identifying marks of the syndrome as well. It's a model that has served us well in medicine for decades.

For mental illnesses, the standard compendium of symptoms, syndromes, and diagnoses is the Diagnostic and Statistical Manual, Version Four, Text Revision, or the DSM-IV-TR (I know – it sounds like someone ate a dictionary and then started burping the alphabet. Not my fault—I just report this stuff, I don't name it. I'd have probably called it the Big Book of Mental Ilnesses, or the BBMI for short.) (American Psychatric Association, 2000). The DSM-IV-TR is just the latest of a series of such manuals that started with the original DSM. But the first two were pretty useless--only since the DSM-III have the manuals actually lived up to their promise and become useful for diagnosing illnesses. (For an interesting article on the origins of the DSM-1, see Grob, 1991.)

Note that this process of listing the symptoms of various syndromes and then giving the syndromes names isn't the same as explaining them or suggesting treatments. We aren't necessarily talking about what causes the symptoms, and, in the case of mental illnesses, we often don't actually know. The cause of symptoms is referred to, in medical terms, as the "etiology." Most mental illnesses have multiple causes or etiologies, just like many physical illnesses do.

Identifying a syndrome is certainly a first step toward discovering an etiology, but it's only a first step. Yet people often mistakenly think that by naming something we've come to understand that thing, or even that we now know what to do about it. Let's say Uncle Lutwidge starts drinking every day at 11 AM and drinks himself into a stupor every night. Your know-it-all cousin proclaims, "It's obvious why he drinks like that – he's an alcoholic!" But that's not an explanation, it's just a convenient shorthand for all his symptoms, a name for a syndrome. You've not come a bit closer to explaining his behavior, you've only named it. (I run into students all the time who are thinking of careers in psychology who have troubled themselves to memorize the Latin names of various phobias. "Oh, you're afraid of spiders," they say. "You obviously have arachnophobia!" Then they lean back with a satisfied smirk, certain they've gotten to the root of your fear. But they haven't gotten even one step nearer to explaining your problem. They've merely named it in a dead language. They're saying you're afraid of spiders because you're afraid of spiders.)

So the DSM-IV-TR attempts to be a comprehensive list of symptoms of mental illnesses, such that we can use those symptoms to give illnesses names. How did this particular categorization system come into being to start with? How do we know which symptoms, when found together, indicate presence of which illnesses? The illness classifications on the DSM are chosen by committees of psychiatrists, who search through research articles dealing with each illness, read what symptoms and characteristics have been found to be associated with each illness, sometimes do some research of their own, and then vote on what to include and what not to include in the final diagnostic criteria, based on whatever personal judgment they care to bring to bear.

For example, the DSM-IV-TR criteria for attention deficit hyperactivity disorder specify that, in order to be diagnosed as having ADHD, the individual should show six or more symptoms in two different categories. The two categories are symptoms of inattention and symptoms of hyperactivity-impulsivity, and the six or more symptoms have to be scattered between them. In addition, the symptoms have to be present before age seven, the symptoms have to be present in two or more physical locations, they must cause significant impairment of functioning, and the symptoms can't be due to another mental disorder. The particular types of inattention and hyperactivity-impulsivity listed by the DSM were chosen by the committee for ADHD based on their readings of current research in ADHD, and the number of symptoms one has to show were also chosen by that committee.

Which probably leaves you wondering, why six symptoms? Why not five or seven? Is there really any appreciable difference between people who show five symptoms and those who show six? And how does the severity of the symptoms fit into the diagnosis? Wouldn't five clear and vivid symptoms be more indicative of this mental illness than seven somewhat more vague and less vivid symptoms? Also, how severe do the symptoms have to be before we say they cause "significant" impairment of functioning? How different do the settings of the symptoms have to be before we can say they're clearly appearing in two or more settings? Are your home and your best friend's house different enough, or do we need the settings to be more different, such as your house and school, or your bedroom and Grand Central Station? Why do the symptoms have to occur before age 7? Why not age 6 or age 8? Should we really exclude a child from ADHD diagnosis because we didn't see any symptoms until he was 85 months old? What do we do if we're doing a diagnosis in retrospect, and we know nothing of the person's childhood beyond their rather dubious memories and the even less trustworthy memories of their loving relatives?

In the end, it's a matter of judgment on the part of the person making the diagnosis whether an individual's symptoms are vivid enough and significant enough and occurred early enough to qualify the person as meeting diagnostic criteria. When the symptoms are many and vivid and fit the illness symptoms exactly, diagnosis isn't that difficult, and there are certainly cases like that. The child who continuously bounces off the walls in every setting, is so wildly impulsive that he seems out of control, and is both flunking out of school and unable to participate in other childhood activities is an easy ADHD diagnosis. But for every such child, there are far greater numbers of cases involving children whose symptoms aren't so vivid and whose fit to the criteria is more marginal.

It's important to make an accurate diagnosis, too, because the treatments commonly used for ADHD aren't to be taken lightly. Most people diagnosed with ADHD take drugs for the condition on a daily basis. Behavior treatments such as behavioral modification can be used, but such treatments are generally expensive, not readily available, and by themselves may not be suitable for the most heavily afflicted. The two drugs most commonly used are mild stimulants: Ritalin and Adderall. It often surprises people that children who can't sit still are given drugs that would, on the surface, appear to make them even more active. Physicians used to say that such stimulants have a "paradoxical effect," because their effect is to calm hyperactive children down. It is now recognized that this effect isn't paradoxical at all -- the stimulants appear to heighten activity in the brain's frontal lobes and limbic system. This makes those sections of the brain, necessary for control of impulses and for focusing attention, active enough that patients can clamp down on inappropriate actions and focus their thoughts without losing track of what they are doing. Ritalin and Adderall aren't particularly powerful drugs, and their stimulating effects aren't massive. But they're still stimulants, and that means they make it harder for users to sleep soundly and may cause loss of appetite, restlessness, nervousness, and dry mouth. You don't want to fling drugs around with wild abandon, you want to make your diagnosis with care (I'm not sure that you should fling anything around with wild abandon these days, not with the way people file lawsuits at the drop of a hat).

So who's making the judgment of whether the person's symptoms are sufficient to meet the criteria of the DSM-IV-TR or some variant of it, and how do they decide who has ADHD and who doesn't? For most people, it's family physicians, whereas for some others it's specialists in childhood disorders. In both cases, judging whether the patient fits the symptoms or not is tricky, because we're not making those judgments against an absolute scale. To determine if a child has ADHD, we need to see how well he can do various attention tasks compared to the rest of the population of children his age, because it's normal for children's attentional abilities to improve with age. But it's not just a matter of putting the child into category A, "normal," or category B, "ADHD." It's actually quite difficult to determine where the category of normal ends and the category of abnormal begins in this case.

The gradual transition between people who are considered "low normals" and those who are diagnosed with ADHD occurs because ability to focus attention isn't caused by just one factor that might be present or absent. When characteristics are caused by just one factor, we end up with two separate groups in the population, those who have the condition and those who don't. For example, if you possess the gene for 6 fingers and toes, you'll be born with six fingers and toes, and if you have no such genes, you won't. This characteristic splits the population into two distinct groups with no overlap between them. (If I had 6 toes, I'd become a surfer just so I could say "I hung twelve out there today!"). Categories such as this pair are called "discrete," because you're either in one category or the other, with no middle ground in between. You could also call these categories "dichotomous," because they involve two discrete, non-overlapping choices.

Ability to focus attention is neither discrete nor dichotomous. Ability to focus attention is a trait affected by many factors, including multiple genes, current blood sugar levels, the amount of stress one is currently under, one's childhood experiences, reward and punishment contingencies, and a whole host of other factors. Each of these possibly hundreds of contributing factors may be present or absent. Generally, when a human ability is affected by many factors that can be present or absent, it tends to be found to be distributed according to what lay people often call a "bell curve" and would probably be more accurately called "the normal distribution."

The normal distribution is actually the logical end product of a simple idea with complicated connotations, a little thing many college statistics students learn about called the "binomial distribution." The binomial distribution merely describes what happens when we have an event occur multiple times or multiple events occur that have two possible outcomes. Let us say, for example, that we're merely flipping a coin to observe what sorts of outcomes we might expect. If we were to flip the coin once, there are two possible outcomes – heads or tails, with the coin having about a 50-50 chance of coming up one way or the other. Suppose, though, that we flip the coin twice. Now there are four possible results, heads and then heads again, heads and then tails, tails and then heads, and tails and then tails again. So there is a one out of four chance of tossing two heads, a one out of four chance of tossing two tails, and a two out of four chance of tossing one of each. If you were to graph that binomial outcome of 2 tosses, your distribution would look like this:

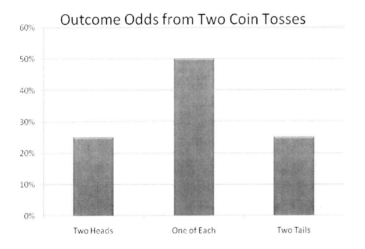

Now let us suppose we toss the coin 3 times. There are 8 possible results of our flips: H-H-H, H-H-T, H-T-H, T-H-H, H-T-T, T-H-T, T-T-H, and T-T-T. So the odds of throwing three heads is one out of eight, the odds of throwing three tails is also one out of eight. There are three combinations that result in two heads and a tail, so the odds of throwing two heads and a tail is three out of eight. And there are also three combinations that result in two tails and a head, so the odds of throwing two tails and a head is also three out of eight. Graphing the outcomes of that series of tosses gives us a distribution that looks like this:

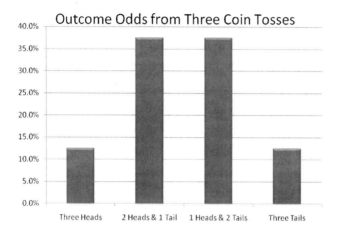

Now if we throw the coin four times, there are sixteen possible results of our flips – H-H-H-H, H-H-H-T, H-H-T-H, H-T-H-H, T-H-H-H, T-H-H-T, H-H-T-T, H-T-H-T, H-T-T-H, T-H-T-H, T-T-H-H, T-T-T-H, T-T-H-T, T-H-T-T, H-T-T-T, and T-T-T-T. (I know this is getting tedious – I promise this will be the last one). So there is only one combination of four heads, and we have a one out of sixteen chance of that outcome. There is also only one combination of four tails, so we have only a one out of sixteen chance for that outcome as well. There are four outcomes of three heads and a tail, and four outcomes with three tails and a head, so each of those have a four out of sixteen or one out of four chance of occurring. And there are six outcomes with two heads and two tails, so two heads and two tails has a six out of sixteen chance of occurring, or three out of eight. The distribution of the possible outcomes looks like this:

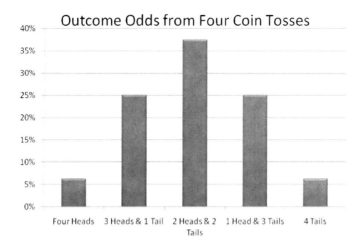

Skipping the calculations, which I'm pretty sure you can do on your own if you're interested, here is the table of outcomes for 5 coin tosses:

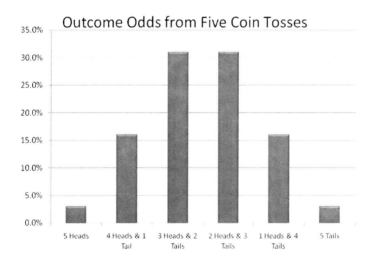

And here is the outcome for 6:

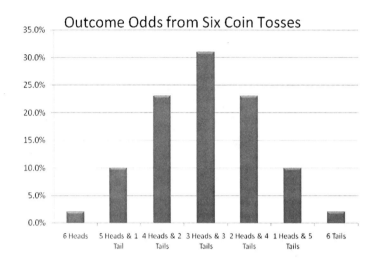

And, finally, if you were to flip a coin 7 times, here's the outcome chart, and the odds of each outcome:

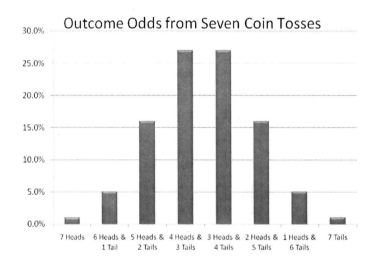

You could keep flipping the coin more and more times, and constructing new tables of outcomes, demonstrating to all the world that you've got way too much time on your hands, but the trend is already clear. There are some rare events out at the edge of the distribution, such as getting all heads or all tails, and some much more common events in the center of the distribution, where approximately equal proportions of heads and tails occur, and that pattern doesn't change as we flip the coin more and more times, it just makes a smoother, more detailed curve. So what if we flipped the coin not once or four times or even seven, but hundreds or thousands of times? What if we flipped the coin an infinite number of times?

As the number of times we flip the coin increases, the distribution gets steadily smoother, but its general shape doesn't change. Keep flipping the coin more and more times and it gradually approaches the bell curve or normal distribution I referred to above. The normal distribution earned its "bell curve" appellation—it looks very much like a bell, as you can see in the example below. You can also see that the binomial distributions we described above were gradually headed toward the general form of this distribution.

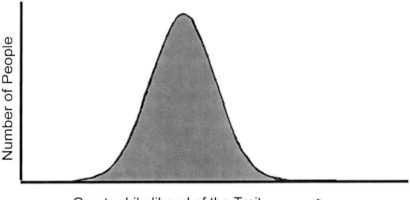

Now let's consider a trait such as ability to focus attention. Ability to focus attention is probably affected by hundreds or thousands of small influences, each of which can be present or absent. So the presence or absence of each trait is much like getting heads or tails each time you flip the coin. There are hundreds, perhaps thousands of such influences making the focus of attention either easier or harder. So if we graph the ability of humans of a given age to focus attention, we'd probably end up with a normal distribution, just like the example above:

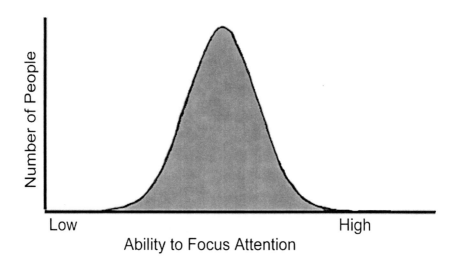

As you can see, there are a large number of people with an average ability to focus attention, with progressively fewer people as we go to higher and higher or lower and lower attention- focusing skills. That's because the odds a given person will possess a mixture of factors, some of which increase and some of which decrease ability to focus attention, is quite likely, just like having a mixture of heads and tails is quite likely. But having almost all or all of the factors be in favor of ability to focus attention or against ability to focus attention isn't as likely, any more than getting almost all or all heads, or almost all or all tails is likely when you flip a coin. It happens now and then, but don't bet the farm on it.

Now, let us suppose that the mundane tasks a person usually performs in day-to-day life require a certain ability to focus attention. We'll draw a line on the graph at that particular point. We'll designate as "normal" people with that level of ability or greater, and we'll designate as "abnormal" everyone with a lower level of ability, because they don't have the ability it takes to do the mundane tasks of life.

Ah, but where should we draw that line? How bad at focusing attention does one have to be before we're willing to say their abilities are abnormally low? Does one have to be in the bottom 1%? Or are people who are in the bottom 2%, or 5%, or 8%, or 10% also abnormally low? Traditionally, medical people have designated the range of normality for a variety of traits as being between the 5th and 95th percentiles of the population. So people who are in the lowest 5% of the population are considered abnormally low on that quality, and those in the top 5% are abnormally high. For example, children who are in the bottom 5% of the population in height are considered abnormally short, and those in the top 5% are considered abnormally tall. Those between these two points are considered normal.

So let's do what medical people have routinely done, and draw a line between the bottom 5% of the population and the rest of the population in our graph of ability to focus attention. We're only marking the bottom 5% of the population as abnormal on ability to focus attention, because, frankly, ability to focus attention at an abnormally high level really isn't a liability of any kind, even though it's still rare and mildly weird. (I was one of those kids, and believe me, I was rare and mildly weird. Perhaps more than mildly weird, but that's another story.) Now our graph looks like this:

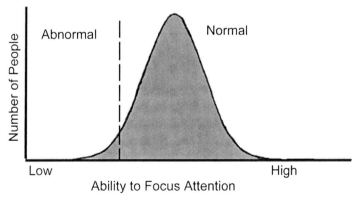

People above the dividing line are said to have normal levels of ability to focus attention, and those below the dividing line will be classified as abnormally low in ability to focus attention, and thus candidates for meeting the DSM-IV-TR criteria for ADHD. (You may have noticed a discrepancy here from something mentioned at the beginning of the chapter, in that according to how this dividing line was chosen 5% of the population should have ADHD, but in fact as I pointed out in the opening paragraphs, about 7.5% of the population is actually diagnosed with ADHD. More about that later.)

Who makes this decision of whether the person is in this bottom 5% or not? It's up to the skill of the examiner to make this judgment. You would hope that he or she had seen lots of normally focused as well as abnormally-focused kids, so that he or she would have a representative group for comparison. If our diagnostician does, it's just a matter of determining where your child falls compared to other children his or her age and the diagnosis of normal or abnormal can be made. Sounds straightforward, right?

It is, if the child is well above or well below the dividing line. But what if he or she is almost on top of the line? Is our diagnostician that reliable and accurate that he or she will consistently be able to tell who's on the normal side of the line and who isn't? I wouldn't bet on it, even in the case of the most skilled diagnosticians, because the differences in behavior on either side of the line are too subtle. Also, most diagnosticians don't see that many normal kids – they see a whole lot of abnormal kids instead, because people seldom bring normal kids in to be diagnosed. That's bound to color their judgments.

The difficulty of separating the people at the borderline becomes even more critical because, as you can see by looking at our normal distribution above, there are more people whose abilities to focus attention are right below and right above the dividing line between ADHD and normal than there are in the more extreme, easily diagnosed group that is found far below that line.

Now let's add another complication (I know how much all of you love a good complication, so I try to oblige your desires whenever possible). I'll do it by raising another question. Why did we draw our line at the 5% point, anyway? Why not 6%, or 4%, or 8%, or 3%? I ask this question of my classes all the time, and they generally look at me blankly (You haven't lived until you've had several hundred people stare at you blankly all at the same time. It makes you question your whole reason for being. On the other hand, it beats people looking at you hungrily with eating utensils in their hands). When I ask the question of why we draw the line at 5%, eventually someone suggests it's because that's the criterion we've always used in medicine, so that must be the right way to do it.

"That's the way we've always done it" is pretty much never a very informative answer to a question, and it isn't in this case, either. But there was a reason that number was chosen originally, a reason that had nothing to do with quality of diagnosis, nor with good medical practice. The reason we draw this arbitrary line at the 5% point is because we have ten appendages on our hands – eight fingers and two thumbs (take a minute and count them if you don't believe me. You'll find ten of them, unless you're one of those freaky 6-fingered people I talked about earlier, or you've had an unfortunate encounter with a kitchen or workshop appliance or a sickle mower). Because we have ten digital appendages, we use a base ten counting system, where ten ones make one ten, ten tens make one one-hundred, ten one-hundreds make one-thousand, and so on. Because we have ten appendages, we count by tens. Because we count by tens, we designate 10% of the population overall as being abnormal, the 5% that's too high on the quality and the 5% that's too low. It's very much an arbitrary number. If we had three fingers and a thumb like Homer Simpson, Bugs Bunny, and all the other toons, we'd probably use a base 8 number system, and undoubtedly have drawn our arbitrary line determining those who are abnormally low at the 4% point.

But does it really matter all that much that the line is largely arbitrary? Let's consider those people who are on the immediate opposite sides of this arbitrary line between normal and abnormal.

These individuals really aren't different from each other in any meaningful way; however, those whose ability to focus is slightly higher than the dividing line are considered "low normal," whereas those whose ability to focus is slightly lower than the dividing line are thought of as "abnormal." The distinction we're making between these two groups is artificial. The truth of the matter is, different situations require different levels of attention. Staying focused while listening to a boring lecture in a classroom may require much higher levels of attention than listening to a guide while on an interesting field trip, where staying focused is fairly easy. Even having a more interesting teacher may make a child seem normal one year, and switching to a more boring teacher may make him seem a victim of ADHD the next year. What we end up with is not a neat line distinguishing normal from abnormal, but rather a whole range of lines, drawn in different places on the distribution, depending on who's drawing the line and just what the child is being asked to do. Thus, two children with identical abilities to focus attention could be classified quite differently because of who's evaluating them, and in what surroundings. Unfair though it sounds, the child's environmental demands have quite a lot to do with whether he or she will be classified as abnormal or not.

Thomas Szasz raised this issue back in 1960 in his famous article *The Myth of Mental Illness.* You can read his actual original APA article in its entirety at this web site: http://psychclassics.yorku.ca/Szasz/myth.htm. In this article and his other writings, Szasz pointed out that some behaviors that are classified as abnormalities would probably be more properly classified as "problems in living." The difference between the two designations is a significant one. Calling a behavior or set of behaviors "abnormal" suggests that the problem is with the individual, and only the individual. He or she is inadequate or functions insufficiently compared to how he or she should function. But if we say he or she has "problems in living," we're suggesting that the difficulty is his or her fit to society and the expectations of that society at that moment, rather than solely in the person himself. We still might treat the individual, but we don't *blame* him or her.

ADHD provides a classic example of just what Szasz meant. The children with the very lowest abilities to focus attention probably wouldn't be able to function well in any human society. Yet those who are slightly higher, especially those right on the borderline of the arbitrary line we've drawn at the 5th percentile, probably could function quite well in some societies. Sadly for them, in many industrial societies, we expect those children to sit still in schools and learn a lot of intellectual material through direct teaching rather than experience or physical activity. Children with difficulty focusing attention are strongly challenged by such a requirement.

Let's picture an ancient hunter-gatherer tribe of humans on the African savannas of antiquity for a moment. A group of youngsters are being taught important tracking and hunting skills. Most of this instruction is going to involve a short demonstration followed by practice. The children will be shown the signs to look for and how to seek them, and then they'll be told to practice doing what they've been shown. They'll be shown how to cast a spear with a spear slinger, and then they'll practice casting. The verbal instructions involved in these vital survival skills, the parts where you have to hold still and pay close attention, are bound to be limited. The demonstration part of the lesson and the practice part of it will make up the bulk of learning.

Now let's say little Og can't focus his attention for more than a minute or two at a time, whereas little Ug can focus attention for hours without his attention wandering. Either way, it really isn't going to matter much, because no one is being asked to focus longer than a minute or two before going off to practice. And if, during practice, Og's attention wanders, Ug will probably focus him again by making him the target of the next toss of his (hopefully blunted) spear. And once the boys are out in the wild, Og's lack of ability to focus attention might work to his advantage—unlike Ug, he won't be so intent on following a track that he doesn't notice anything else. Instead, his attention will keep leaving the track, and thus it will be Og who first notices the lion crouched in the brush, hoping to pick off a tasty human treat, and Og who saves Ug from dying of his own intense attentional focus. In fact, if you consider it, having a mixture of abilities to focus attention in the hunting group gives us balance – we've got people to keep the others focused and on task, and people who are easily distracted and notice when things aren't as they should be.

But put Og and Ug in a modern day classroom, and everything changes. Now there is no advantage at all in Og's wandering attention that makes him perhaps the first to notice something on the periphery isn't right. Only Ug's ability to focus attention even in a hurricane is advantageous here. Most of the children identified as having ADHD in our society would probably have gotten along just fine in a society that was more action-based, especially those on the margin with normalcy. Is it fair to call such children "abnormal?" or is it our expectation that they will sit still that is at fault?

If you're on the borderline, whether you get diagnosed with ADHD and medicated or not is pretty much a crapshoot (If you're not reading the chapters in order, I invite you to refer to Chapter 2, *Linguistic Superstition*, for a discussion of shooting craps, the origin of the term "crap," and other such mildly scatological issues). Some parents bring in children who are simply low normals when it comes to ability to focus attention, but describe those children's symptoms so vividly that they give the diagnosing physicians the impression that their children are more active and impulsive than they are and in more circumstances, resulting in those children receiving an ADHD diagnosis and a prescription for stimulants. This is one of the reasons that ADHD diagnoses, as reported by the Mayo clinic in the first paragraph of the chapter, are actually half again as common as our target 5%. Desperate parents and teachers sometimes almost demand a diagnosis of abnormality, and physicians and diagnosticians are sometimes swayed by such pressures. A different child, who has teachers and parents more tolerant of disarray and chaos, may not even be considered for diagnosis. Yet that child's ability to focus attention may be much lower than the first child's.

A final note about Attention Deficit Hyperactivity Disorder. Children who are at the very bottom of the distribution of ability to focus attention are completely unambiguous. As Barbara Henker of UCLA has pointed out, such children do not function well in most environments, and stimulant drugs may be a necessity for their successful development and well-being (Henker & Whalen, 1989). But children just to either side of the normal/abnormal borderline may be better served by giving children more freedom to move during school days, engaging them with more stimulating learning techniques, and being more tolerant of a little bit of distraction and disorder.

Reading Disorder (Dyslexia)

Reading disorder, the condition formally known as dyslexia, is also an excellent example of a disorder that would better be considered a problem in living rather than a mental illness. As was the case with ability to focus attention, reading skill is normally distributed, with the bulk of people hovering around average in ability and with increasingly smaller numbers of people who are incredibly good or incredibly bad at reading. As was the case with ADHD, we draw an arbitrary line on the distribution of abilities, and then label everyone who is below that line as being abnormal.

Psychologists and psychiatrists changed the designation for people who have otherwise normal intelligence but who seem to have abnormal difficulty in learning to read from "dyslexia" to "reading disorder" when the DSM-IV replaced the DSM-III-R. Those on the committee looking at reading disorder were undoubtedly driven by many motivations for their choice. But one was almost certainly losing all the negative baggage the term "dyslexia" had acquired over the years. Giving the syndrome such a straightforward English name also helped deal with the belief that many people have that giving something a Latin name explains it. "Little Lutwidge seems intelligent and does okay at math," the parent tells the diagnostician, "but he can't seem to read at all." After conducting a variety of tests, our diagnostician sits down with the parents and says, gravely, "I have determined your child is dyslexic."

"Oh, that explains it! That's why he's a bad reader!" the parents sigh in relief. "He's a bad reader because he has dyslexia!" But all we've done is give his syndrome a name -- "Dys" is a Latin prefix that means "bad," and "lexia" means "reading," so the term "dyslexia" means, quite literally, "bad reading." To say Lutwidge is a bad reader because he's dyslexic is simply saying he's a bad reader because he's a bad reader.

Like many syndromes, including ADHD, reading disorder has multiple causes. In fact, many people mistake one of its symptoms for a cause. Most people with reading disorder will write words from right to left rather than left to right at times, and will also attempt to read them that way. Sometimes they'll also mistake "d's" for "b's" and "p's" for "q's." Seeing this, many people assume that dyslexics have problems in reading because they seeing things backwards. I and many other psychologists only wish that was the case. Think about it – if reading disorder was just a matter of children seeing things backwards, we could give them prism glasses to wear when reading that simply flipped everything the other direction, and we could simply set up their computers to mirror image all text.

But reading disorder isn't as simple as children seeing words and letters backwards. In this case, we've got a directionality problem. Our relationship goes the other way – children with reading disorder don't have trouble reading because they confuse directions of letters and words. Instead, they confuse the directions of letters and words because they have trouble reading.

Normal children routinely do the same thing when first learning to read. Years ago, when my children were very young, my wife and I used to bring them to night classes when we were talking about Jean Piaget's work, and ask the children questions and have them do things so the students could see how children reason differently from adults. One of those nights we arrived a bit early. My son

Matt, who as a preschooler was just learning to write his name, spotted the white board and the markers and made a bee-line for them, where he quite proudly wrote his name. He started on the right, probably because that's where the marker had been sitting, so as he wrote he moved to the left, spelling his name out beautifully (and backwards) in big, clumsy block letters.

One of the students in back looked up and saw him beaming at the rest of us with an open marker in his hand, regarding his handiwork. "Oh, my gosh!" she blurted. "Your son's dyslexic! That must be so difficult, you guys being professors and all!"

Every child defense instinct in me rushed to the fore, but before I could think of something intelligent (and probably rude and ill advised) to say, my wife Andrea beat me to it. "He's not dyslexic," she said, fixing the woman with a glare that could have turned stone molten. "He's four." She was right, of course. All unskilled readers and writers have trouble with left-right distinctions initially, because they're difficult, and they're arbitrary. As children become more skilled at literary tasks, they stop having such problems. Children with reading disorder continue to show such problems as a symptom of their disorder, not its cause.

So what causes reading disorder? Many, many things. Different things in different people. Some people seem to have problems linking the visual shapes of letters and words with their meanings, possibly because of connection problems between the occipital lobes in the back of the brain, where vision is processed, and the temporal lobes (surprisingly enough, in the temples) where language is processed. These people are sometimes said to have "surface dyslexia."

Other people have what is called "phonological dyslexia," where their difficulty is in connecting the shapes of words and letters to their sounds. These people often can learn to read fluently by learning to sight-recognize words rather than sound them out. The inability to link sights of letters and their sounds slows them down, though, because sounding out words often is one of the ways we learn to read initially, and a way we can teach ourselves words even when others aren't around to help us. Normal people lean heavily on phonetic decoding, or "phonics" to learn to read initially, largely abandoning it as they become skilled readers who've memorized words by sight. But while they're learning, they find phonics a handy tool, one that is denied to those with phonetic dyslexia.

There are lots of other causes of reading disorders as well. Some children can read readily if words are presented one at a time in isolation, but can't read them when surrounded by other words, which is probably an attentional problem. Some can read words when they're presented as yellow text on a green background, or white text on a black background. I could go on, but you get the picture. The diagnosis of reading disorder simply tells us the child has trouble reading and it's not due to overall mental retardation – it doesn't tell us the actual cause.

Some have even suggested that the largest group of "dyslexics" are people with reasonably normal abilities and normally-acting neural systems who have just had too little experience in reading to read fluently and thus lag behind their peers. Reading is an automatized skill, an ability like many others that becomes better with practice. With enough practice, we eventually get so good at it that it happens without conscious thought. In fact, reading is so automatic that you can't look at a word and not read it once you've become fluent. (Try it some time. Sometimes I pull down the projector screen in a classroom and write a phrase, then instruct my class to look at a phrase when I raise the screen but not to read it. The phrase I write is "I knew you'd read it anyway," and it never fails).

Reading skill is strongly dependent on practice initially, and some children just don't get that much practice. They live in households where no one actually reads, no one reads to them, and where televisions and video games run practically 24 hours a day. Why don't they learn to read in school, you ask? The average first grade class has 20 children in it. Even if half the school day is devoted to reading, that's only about 160 to 180 minutes, or about 8-9 minutes of individual attention per child each day, and a variable number of minutes reading along with other children in the rare situations where the child feels inclined to do that rather than just listen, look out the window, or kick the chair in front of him. By contrast, other children have parents who read to them and work on reading every night, giving them enormous amounts of extra practice. Is it any wonder wide differences appear in children's reading abilities by third grade?

I firmly believe, and I tell all my classes, that it's really not the job of the schools to teach your child to read—as a parent, you have more time, and you can give your child one-on-one attention. Even children with reading disorder often improve when given intense practice, and many will eventually read well enough to get by in life, or sometimes even read fluently.

Here again, though, we have the two problems that ADHD diagnoses also share. The cutoff point for diagnosis, the line between normal and abnormal, is arbitrary at best, and more people will be near that arbitrary line than at the more clear-cut extremes of the distribution. And the problem of reading disorder isn't a problem of the individual, it's a problem of living. Little Og and Ug didn't have this problem living a hunter-gatherer life on the savannahs, they probably didn't even have written language, which is a rather modern invention that may only go back about 5000 years. Even as recently as a hundred years ago there were many niches in society for complete illiterates, and people who couldn't use written language could simply rely upon those who could for most purposes. Only in the late 20th century did the need for universal literacy make inability to read well a disorder.

People with extreme difficulty focusing attention, and people who have extreme difficulties learning to read are certainly different from the rest of the population, down on the dysfunctional tail of the normal distribution rather than in the comfortable center or the prestigious upper tail that is the realm of the fortunate and gifted. By putting those variations on a diagnostics manual for mental illnesses, though, we're not just saying these children and adults are different—it implies that something is "wrong" with these people. We've gone from making an observation to making a judgment. Yet, as I've noted, this judgment is arbitrary at best. People below the 5th percentile and above the 95th percentile of height are equally different from the mass of people near the 50th percentile of the normal distribution. Yet it is only the very short who are branded as abnormal, whereas the very tall are often lauded, admired, and asked to join your company basketball and volleyball teams. Still, what are the real problems with being very short, and from where do they arise? As Szasz would point out, the problems arise not because of the person's height, but because all of our mechanisms, all of our furniture, the heights of steps, and the proportions of all of our constructions are sized for bigger people. The short person isn't a problem and his or her dimensions aren't "wrong," the problem is in his or her interfacing with society. It's a problem in living.

Likewise, when we consider ability to focus attention, no one is concerned for or even notices the children above the 95th percentile, let alone calls them "disordered." Those are the children who are so good at focusing attention that they'll stay on task during a tsunami, an alien invasion, or Armageddon itself. Now when you think about it, that much self-control and focus is so rare as to be just plain creepy, but we don't label it as pathological because it doesn't bother us—it doesn't make them hard to live with, it doesn't interfere with lesson plans, and it doesn't keep them from sitting quietly for hours and doing math problems, allowing a teacher to cope with having way too many students in class. That extreme attentional ability is just as weird, but we don't see it as wrong. So why the rush to judgment at the other end of the spectrum?

We shouldn't be surprised that there are people at the extremes of the normal distribution -- The name of the distribution itself emphasizes that every part of it is "normal." The innocent children who have extreme difficulty focusing attention, or who have a lot more trouble learning to read and take more time to do so are neither wrong nor pathological—they're merely different. They need our help, but not our judgment. They have problems in living. It is in labeling them as "disordered," that we create a wrong. That's not the fault of the makers of the DSM-IV-TR, whose job is simply to describe syndromes, not determine their causes. Like many great tools, the flaw comes in misusing this diagnostic tool, in using it to lay the responsibility for the problem in living on the person, rather than on the interaction between the person's abilities and the demands of the society itself.

References:

Diagnostic and statistical manual of mental disorders, 4th edition, text revision: DSM-IV-TR (2000). Washington, D. C.: The American Psychiatric Association.

Grob, G. N. (1991)   Origins of DSM-I: a study in appearance and reality. *American Journal of Psychiatry, 148,* 421-431

Henker, B., & Whalen, C. K. (1989).   Hyperactivity and attention deficits. *American Psychologist, 44(2),*215-223.

Mayo Clinic Study Examines Frequency Of Attention-Deficit/hyperactivity Disorder (AD/HD). Retrieved from http://www.sciencedaily.com/releases/2002/03/020314080350.htm

Szasz, Thomas. *(1960)* The myth of mental illness. *American Psychologist, 15,* 113-118. Can also be retrieved from http://psychclassics.yorku.ca/Szasz/myth.htm

Chapter 5: I'm Only Using 10% of this Chapter

The only thing we have to fear is fear itself - nameless, unreasoning, unjustified, terror which paralyzes needed efforts to convert retreat into advance.
---- Franklin Delano Roosevelt - First Inaugural Address, March 4, 1933

All of us are born with a set of instinctive fears--of falling, of the dark, of lobsters, of falling on lobsters in the dark, or speaking before a Rotary Club, and of the words "Some Assembly Required."
---- Humor columnist Dave Barry

Every time I teach an introductory psychology class, at some point, usually early on, someone raises the question. "Is it true?" they ask, "that we use only 10% of our brains?" (The percentage itself varies, sometimes lower than 10, sometimes as high as 25%. But it's always an absurdly low number). The question is also expressed in other ways. A very popular version is the hopeful, "Are you going to teach us how to use the parts of the brain we don't normally use?" There's also the "skeptical of science" version, that goes, "Since scientists don't know what 90% of the brain does, how do you know it doesn't do cool stuff like telepathy and ESP?"

The popular belief that we use only portions of our brain has roots that go way back and derives from many sources, and we're going to look at those sources. But the question of what percentage of our brain we use also derives from the unfortunate way we look at this important organ. We call it "the" brain, just like way say "the heart," "the lungs" or "the liver." Like those other important organs, we see the brain as one unit, a single, integrated organ. But the brain isn't really a single organ like that. Unlike the heart and the lungs, it has more than a single function. Unlike the liver, its parts aren't uniform. The parts of the brain are all linked, like the parts of the heart, lungs, and liver, but although they are highly connected and interlocking, the brain is made of specialized modules, with different parts doing different things at the same time. Sometimes, different parts of the brain disagree with each other, leaving it to other parts to resolve the disagreement. That latter issue, where parts of the brain suggest different courses of action that have to be reconciled, we'll consider in a bit. First, though, let's dispose of our original question: Is it true we use only 10% of our brains?

That depends on what you mean when you say we only use 10% of our brains. That statement itself is actually much more vague than the use of a precise percentage would suggest. I can think of three different things a person might mean by this statement just off the top of my head. We might be saying:

- Only 10% of the cells in the brain are involved in thinking or controlling our bodies.

- At any given point only 10% of the brain is in use.

- We only know what 10% of the brain does, and the other 90% has no purpose at all (acting as a kind of "spare" brain), or has an unknown purpose (perhaps doing wondrous things most of us aren't even aware we have the potential to do).

Whether it is true that we use only 10% of our brains or not depends upon which of these interpretations is meant by our questioner. If the speaker means by that statement that only 10% of the cells in the brain are involved in thinking, no psychologist or physiologist is going to disagree. Roughly ninety percent of the cells of the brain aren't neurons, or cells that are used for thinking. They're glial cells, the support cells that make myelin (an important neural insulator) and aid brain cells in obtaining nutrition and surviving. They don't do neural processing, but that doesn't make those cells unimportant. This meaning of the utterance, though, is profoundly uninteresting and unimportant. It's rather like saying we only use 10% of our cars because 90% of the parts aren't involved in moving us down the road but merely serve cooling, oiling, monitoring, and support functions.

If the claim that we only use 10% of our brains is intended to mean that most of the time, only 10% of the processing capacity of the brain is being used, that's probably true as well. Yet it doesn't mean the rest is available for some other grand purpose. After all, you probably are using fewer than 10% of your muscle cells at any given time, too, unless you're doing full body exercise at a furious pace at the moment, and if you were I doubt you'd be reading this at the same time (if you are, my hat is off to you—that's an impressive feat of multitasking). Does that mean you don't use the other 90% of your muscles?

You're probably using only some of the light fixtures in your house at the moment, too, but that doesn't make you don't need that basement stairwell light, especially if you're not fond of rolling down the length of the stairs to land in a bruised tangle at the foot of them covered with cobwebs. Those brain cells that aren't being used do have purposes, even if you're not using them right this second. What we've got is another interpretation of the claim that we only use 10% of our brains that is true but also is not particularly interesting.

It's the third possibility, though, that most people assume when they hear the statement, "we only use 10% of our brains." They interpret it to mean that the function of 90% of the brain is a grand mystery that science can't solve and that only a few special people ever access that mysterious portion. "Just think of what we could do if we could harness that unused brainpower!" they say.

Sadly for people who hope to change their lives by learning to master powerful, previously unused thinking abilities, this third interpretation is demonstrably false. Because of the ready availability of PET scans, fMRIs, and experimental brain scanning methods such as magnetoencephalography, we now can watch the brain in operation, and see what parts "light up" when we're engaged in various tasks. From such studies, it's clear that all parts of the brain serve identifiable purposes, although not simultaneously, of course. None of it is sitting around idle, let alone 90% of it.

Let's do a quick tour of which parts of the brain serve which purposes. There's an easy to remember general rule for keeping track of which part of the brain has which function. In general, neurons coming into the brain from the body pass across the middle of the brain and end up on the surface of the opposite side from which they entered. So sensory and motor neurons from the left side of the body cross over to the surface of the right side of the brain, and those from the right side of the body cross over to the surface of the left side. For example, input from the left ear feeds into the right hemisphere of the brain, and that from the right ear feeds into the left side.

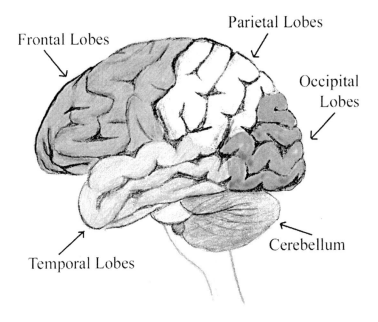

Frontal Lobes

Parietal Lobes

Occipital Lobes

Temporal Lobes

Cerebellum

The large, visible, wrinkled part of the brain that dominates the whole structure is known as the cerebral cortex. It's somewhat separated lengthwise down the middle by a central fissure, creating two hemispheres (But not completely separated, not by a long shot. More about that later). The back parts of these two hemispheres, housed in the part of the skull known as the occipit, are called the occipital lobes. ("Occipit," in Latin, means "opposite the head," because that back part of the skull is directly opposite the front of the head). The occipital lobes are directly opposite the eyes, also, and process visual signals from those eyes as well as containing your memories of how things look. The temporal lobes, surprisingly enough found in the temples on either side of the head, are directly opposite the ears and process auditory signals, as well as containing auditory memories and the section of the brain specialized for language interpretation. That latter section is known as Wernicke's area, and we'll discuss it in a bit, too.

The sections making up the back part of the top of the brain are known as the parietal lobes (the word "parietal" merely means "wall," and the parietal bone in the skull was probably named for the fact that it is the flattest of the bones that fuse to form the skull and most resembles a wall as a consequence). The front-most part of the parietal lobes contain the somatosensory cortex, the section of the brain that processes signals from the touch sensors of the body. Behind that area are where memories for touch are stored, and where spatial information and spatial location is processed. Our knowledge of the shapes of stars and squares is stored there, along with memories of how a sponge feels.

That leaves us with the frontal lobes. The frontal lobes make up the largest section of the cerebral cortex, because humans have huge frontal lobes. The back part of those frontal lobes, right next to the somatosensory cortex, is where motor control originates – it's the part of the brain that actually decides what body parts to move and how to move them. Just ahead of that section is the portion of the frontal lobes that processes motor memories, your memories for how to do things. Also found in the frontal lobes is Broca's area, the section of the brain that takes what Wernicke's area wants to say and actually makes it into speech (we'll talk more about Broca's area later, too).

So much for the back part of the frontal lobes. What about the front-most part of the frontal lobes, often called the prefrontal lobes? The prefrontal lobes are the part of the brain that differs the most between us and our clever cousins, the chimpanzees. Although the rest of the chimpanzee's brain quite strongly resembles our own in size and function, the chimpanzee's frontal lobes are foreshortened compared to ours, sloping off quickly rather than bulging (and this is one case where size definitely matters). Up to 100 years ago or so, many medical researchers were still in the dark concerning just what this huge, bulging overhang above our brows did (other than making our foreheads very tall compared to our ape relatives). If you examined people who'd suffered brain damage to see what abilities they lost, it was clear that people who suffered damage to the occipital lobes had vision problems, those who had damage to parietal lobes lost touch abilities or memories having to do with touch, those who had damage to the back part of the frontal lobes lost motor control abilities, and those who suffered damage to the temporal lobes lost hearing or language abilities. But it was hard sometimes to put a finger on just what abilities were lost when the prefrontal lobes were damaged. That's because the things the prefrontal lobes do are more subtle—they're responsible for impulse control, deductive and abstract reasoning, problem solving, planning—all the things that make us most human.

Some physiologists of 100-plus years ago actually ventured to suggest that the prefrontal lobes were spare tissue that was kept idle, ready to take over if part of the brain was damaged, and these people are probably partially responsible for statement that started this chapter, that we only use 10% of our brains. But modern day physiologists and psychologists know better – these parts of the brain not only are vitally important to our functioning and constantly in use, but they're most responsible for our unique personalities. After all, we don't differ that much from other people in our visual or auditory or tactile (touch) processing, or in the routine motor skills we display. The biggest differences in our personalities are prefrontal lobe issues. Do we resist temptation? Do we plan ahead? Can we engage in complex hypothetical reasoning? Do we look before we leap? Are we quiet or noisy, shy or outgoing, optimistic or pessimistic? All of these are the result of prefrontal lobe functioning, and they're the most important aspects of who we are.

So, in short, every part of our brain has some documented function, and the belief that large parts of it do nothing or do mysterious things we can't comprehend is clearly false. Yet, in one way, there's a grain of truth in the belief that at least tiny parts of our brain were, at least once, more or less unused. To extract that grain of truth, though, to harvest it and thresh it out and grind it into flour so we can make some truth fritters, we need to revert back to our childhoods for a bit.

Let's take a look at the brain of a newborn. Newborns have pretty much all the neurons they're ever going to need in life. Humans only rarely grow whole new neurons after they're born—instead, we lose them at prodigious rates, especially in old age, or when we're on drinking or drug-using binges or crashing our heads into things. It's pretty safe to say that you had more brain cells when you were a newborn than you do now. But having fewer brain cells now is not necessarily a bad thing. Although they have more brain cells than adults, newborns have very few connections between those brain cells. They're like a transportation network that consists only of major superhighways, but with no onramps or connecting roads joining them or leading off the superhighways to anywhere. The trillions of links between neurons found in adults like us, which are responsible for both memories and mental processing, develop throughout life as a result of learning and experience. With life experience, neurons grow connections to other neurons, making those neurons become specialized neurons that do particular tasks. By adolescence, all parts of the brain have specialized functions, and most neurons are in regular use.

But there are neurons that, by the time we've gotten substantially into childhood and sometimes even into adolescence, still aren't serving much purpose. They run in parallel with other neurons connecting more or less the same way as other neurons, but they take microseconds longer to send their signals and thus don't actually do much that's useful. Or they have few unique connections, as other neurons have simply connected around them, thus bypassing them. Having a bunch of neurons sitting around sucking up nutrition and taking up space but not doing much is not an aid to survival, apparently. Because as we get deeper into childhood and finally into adolescence, we start doing something rather shocking. We begin the process of synaptic pruning (Giedd, Blumenthal, Jeffries, Castellanos, Liu, Zijdenbos, et al., 1999).

Synaptic pruning is the process of your body deliberately cutting off neural connections that do little, and killing off neurons that are superfluous. This frees nutrition and resources for neurons that are actually vital and busy, makes room for those neurons to grow more connections and enhance their functioning. In general, then, synaptic pruning speeds up our brains and makes them more efficient. Your neurons have had years in which to demonstrate that they're really needed, and now we're cutting overhead, lowering expenses, and cleaning out the chaff (for a discussion of chaff, see *Chapter 2: Linguistic Superstition*). The net result is that, by our early twenties we have fewer neurons than we did entering our teens, especially fewer useless neurons, and our brains have become lean, mean, thinking machines.

Metaphorically, you could consider the newborn's brain to be like a whole network of computer processers plugged into sockets in motherboards and turned on, sucking up power like crazy, but not connected to keyboards or the Internet or mice or touchscreens, and thus not doing much in the way of useful processing. In childhood we connect those processors up as we need them and give them tasks, and they become specialists with specific abilities. Finally, when it looks like our connection network is done growing, we shut off the processors we're not using and pry them out of the motherboard so we don't waste any more precious power on them. You could consider these neurons that are eventually the victims of synaptic pruning to be "spares," and argue that children only use portions of their brains, and the younger the child, the more accurate that view would be. It's actually fairly hard to determine just how many neurons are removed by synaptic pruning—we can't begin to count the number of neurons we have to start with, so we have to estimate numbers by counting how many neurons are in small sections of the brain and then estimate the total by assuming the density is uniform across the brain (even though we know it isn't). But no one is estimating that anything like 90% of neurons are cut during synaptic pruning, or even half that many. At most, the process may result in a 10% reduction in brain mass, and probably less.

When you think about it, then, the human brain is the very model of efficiency. It even goes so far as to carefully strip out each little neuron and neural connection that isn't used sufficiently by adulthood. Given that's the case, the very idea that we'd have a brain that remains 90% idle is absurd. From an evolutionary standpoint, it also doesn't seem likely that we would carry around that weight of such idle brain tissue, nor waste the energy it would use staying alive. We'd be more susceptible to starvation if we carried around such useless tissue, as well as a bit slower in escaping predators. We'd be at a disadvantage to adults who kept around only the neurons they used, and those adults would have a survival edge. In the interests of survival and efficiency, we use all our brains.

Left Brain, Right Brain

Which brings us to another set of beliefs about the brain that have been repeated so often that people blindly accept it as truth. We're talking about the left-brain, right-brain claims of pop psychology. Most people will tell you the brain is strongly lateralized, and that different people are dominated by different sides of the brain. "I'm a left-brain person," one will say. "I'm logical, verbal, and linear." "Well, I'm a right-brain person," a second will say. "I'm intuitive, holistic, creative, and artistic."   The left brain is supposedly masculine and rational, the right brain feminine and intuitive. Whether you're insulted by these pronouncements depends upon whether you think it is good or bad to be rational or intuitive. (See Williams, 1986, for an example of books making claims like this).

So where did all this left-brain, right-brain stuff come from? It burst into popularity in the 1970's, but its origins go another century back. One can trace the beginnings of the belief in lateralization back to the American Civil War era. In 1861 a French physician named Paul Pierre Broca did an autopsy on a man who, due to the contraction of syphilis, had lost the ability to speak all but a very few words before his death. (Syphilis was known in those days as "The French Pox," even though there's pretty substantial evidence it came from the New World along with tobacco, tomatoes, corn, and Jerusalem artichokes. Life and language are both full of little jokes like this). Broca discovered the now deceased victim of this deadly but misnamed disease had suffered serious damage to an area at the very back part of the left frontal lobe. A later autopsy of a man with a similar loss of ability to speak found similar damage, and Broca proposed that language production was controlled by the back part of the left frontal lobe, a section that became known as "Broca's Area" (Schiller, 1992).

Then in 1874, Carl Wernicke proposed that almost all right-handed people and a good portion of left-handed people do the majority of language understanding and the processing of meaning in the left temporal lobe, in a section of the brain since called "Wernicke's Area." He based that conclusion on studies of people who'd had strokes or accidents that damaged that area. Such people often lost the ability to understand language, and, although they could echo words other people said, they couldn't produce intelligible speech on their own (Eggert, 1977).

Other researchers then found other specialized sections of the brain, and the efforts to map the brain really took off. By the beginning of the 20th century, diagrams existed that assigned functions to pretty much all the sections of the brain, as I've described above. Much of the evidence for what part of the brain did what was collected in the same way that Broca and Wernicke collected their data, by examining people who'd suffered damage to specific parts of the brain, and seeing what abilities they'd lost when the damage occurred. But some of the evidence for which part of the brain did what was also collected in another way, and that data is most responsible for all this left-brain/right-brain nonsense. I'm referring to what we're going to look at next -- the data from the split brain people.

The split brain people we're going to look at did not come about their condition naturally. If you look directly down at the top of a human brain, you'll see that the brain appears to be split into two halves, or hemispheres, with a deep fissure running down the middle. That surface split is rather misleading, though. If you were to poke into it, you'd quickly find that, under that surface fissure, the two halves of the brain are joined together by a group of roughly 80 million neurons running horizontally from the left hemisphere to the right and the right hemisphere to the left, crossing each other in the middle. That thick neural conduit is called the corpus callosum. It ties the left and the right hemispheres of the cerebral cortex tightly together and enables them to work together as a unit.

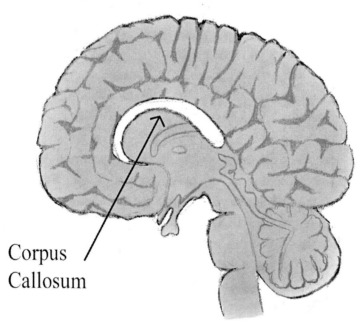

Corpus
Callosum

The corpus callosum is an essential part of the mammalian brain. There are humans who are born with little or no corpus callosum, a condition called agenesis of the corpus callosum (literally, agenesis means, "not born.") These people have severe problems learning motor skills and have motor coordination problems, as well as problems learning patterns, solving complex problems, recognizing people, sensing the emotions of others, and functioning socially. Clearly coordination between the hemispheres hinges on the operation of this important structure.

But back in 1940, a surgeon by the name of William Van Wagenen noted that his patients who were suffering from frequent and uncontrollable grand mal seizures generally had their seizure start in a small portion of damaged brain tissue. Then the seizure readily spread across the corpus callosum to the other hemisphere of the brain, where it would expand and then travel back again, crossing the corpus callosum repeatedly until most of the neurons in the brain were firing in synchrony. Such unnatural synchronous firing of neurons made all conscious thought cease, and the victim collapse and convulse. Van Wagenen hypothesized that severing the corpus callosum would stop the seizure from spreading like wildfire back and forth from one side of the brain to the other. So he severed the connection between the hemispheres in some of these patients, and he found that the number and severity of these people's seizures diminished markedly.

But the treatment was not without its side effects. The severing of the corpus callosum reduced considerably the ability of each half of the brain to communicate with the other. (It didn't eliminate such communication – the two brain hemispheres both share the brain stem, the thalamus, the hypothalamus, and the cingulate gyrus, and many connections go through those structures from one side of the brain to the other. But inter-hemispheric communication diminished considerably in these split-brain people as a result of their operations. As an unintended side effect, this severing of the corpus callosum also made it possible to observe the abilities of each hemisphere at least semi-independently.

Roger Wolcott Sperry tested 10 of Van Wagenen's patients. One thing that he and his colleagues had the split brain people do is to reach into a sack and feel an object, then try to name the object or try to draw it. It was discovered that, if the person felt the object with the right hand, he could usually name it readily, but he could not then remove that hand and draw a picture of the object. But if he felt the object with his left hand, he was unable to name it at all, yet he could draw a picture of it with that hand when he removed it from the bag. As we mentioned earlier, signals from the left hand cross over to the right side of the brain and vice-versa. So feeling things with the right hand meant the left hemisphere was the portion naming them, and feeling things with the left hand meant that the right hemisphere was appreciating the spatial relations between parts of the objects. These results, and other like them, led Sperry to conclude that the hemispheres of the brain experienced and processed different aspects of experience, with most verbal processing occurring in the left hemisphere, and spatial processing in the right (Erdmann & Stover, 2000).

Pop psychology took these rather limited and preliminary results and ran with them. And we're not talking about just a little jog in the same direction, we're talking, wild, abandoned, uncontrolled, Forrest Gump-type hoofing. We reason verbally, the pop psychologists said, so the left hemisphere must be logical and rational. Artists use spatial information, so the right hemisphere, which does much spatial processing, must be intuitive and artistic. It was just a short jump from there to the conclusion that different personality types are dominated by different hemispheres. From there, the left-brain, right-brain people jumped to the idea that we can train ourselves to be more "right brained," or "left brained."

In the end, all this running and jumping took us a long way from a bit of fairly simple data collected by Sperry on ten very, very odd individuals. And we must make no mistake about it, the split brain people are very odd individuals. Yes, their processing shows pretty extreme levels of hemispheric differentiation, with one hemisphere doing one set of tasks, and the other doing others. But the wide separation of left and right brain functions that Sperry found in Van Wagenen's patients found may itself be a product of the fact that those patients are, indeed, split brain individuals, and not normal people. It's important to keep two things in mind in particular when we consider drawing conclusions from split brain research to the functioning of our own brains – these people had brain functioning problems to start with that suggest the presence of brain abnormalities, and each the rest of us have an intact corpus callosum, and these people don't.

That intact corpus callosum means that your normal brain operates as a unit, not as two partially disconnected hemispheres. Whatever integrated processing the split brain people might have done initially, the severing of the giant neural trunk that joined the two halves of their cerebral cortex put an end to it. It isn't terribly surprising, then, that Sperry found some pretty extreme differences in the functioning of the hemispheres. The operation itself would have made such differences more extreme, even if they were mild to start with.

Consider this metaphor for a moment. You're sitting at your computer, and you connect through your high speed Internet connection to the World Wide Web. That means that your computer has the ability to address one of the server computers that is connected to the backbone of the web somewhere in the world. That server's connections, then, allow you to connect to all the other computers that connect to that web backbone, just as if they were an extension of your computer. Once you do, you can call up the web in all its glory, from manuals on how to set the clock on your ancient VCR to newsfeeds from Thailand to adult sites you'd probably rather I didn't mention around your relatives and coworkers. All of them can be seen just as if they were stored on your computer and were being retrieved directly by it, even though they're actually being processed by some other computer that is located in some empty server room who knows where. It doesn't really matter which computer has which information or is executing which code, because they're all linked together.

So let's say that you're writing a technical manual for your company's new product, the Handy-Dandy Dust Bunny Fluffer (buy one now and we'll throw in the dryer lint attachment, a smokeless ashtray, and a knife so sharp it can cut through a tin can and still slice a tomato or trim a Jerusalem artichoke). Your technical people, who have the diagrams for the controls and the other critical parts of this wondrous device, have stored them for you in a folder on a computer in Bora Bora, where said technical people live and work. The information you need on how to contact customer service (and believe me, they're going to need customer service for this baby) is stored on the company tech service web site in Walla Walla. The introductory greeting and personal message thanking the customer for buying the product is being written by the company vice president, who is doing it in her spare time while vacationing in Pago Pago. (Why she went to American Samoa for a vacation instead of somewhere a bit more scenic I can't say--just bear with me here, I've almost gotten to the point). And lastly, the set of specs for the HDDBF is in a corporate database in Obi Obi.

So you start writing your tech manual. Periodically, you pull pieces that you need from all these far flung places, where they're stored on machinery other than your own. But because you're connected to that machinery, and your computer knows the addresses of each of those machines and is connected to it, it's just as if that information was right there in your machine. You're assembling it, but the pieces are elsewhere. Because the Internet is up and running, and all the essential computers are also running and connected to it, which hardware is processing which particular part doesn't matter.

Now suppose your connection to the Internet fails, the equivalent of severing your computer's corpus callosum joining it to the rest of the computer brains out in the world. Without access to the Internet and your list of net locations to pull the information together, those separate parts will just sit there, stored in those distant machines, out of reach and inaccessible. You could go ahead and write the manual on your machine, but you'd not have access to the portions of it that are stored elsewhere, so your manual would be a stunted thing with only linguistic material in it, no pictures, diagrams or other spatial materials. For that matter, even some of the linguistic material, the forward from your Vice President, is now unreachable, and thus cannot be joined to the rest of the linguistic material you have on your computer. People who, unlike you, are still connected to the Internet, might stumble across the address of the pictures and diagrams on the computer in Bora Bora, but without your accompanying written files they won't be able to identify or use them. The system that had operated as a smoothly coordinated unit seconds ago due to its inter-connective links is now a bunch of separate capabilities, and the unit that coordinated them is now on the other side of that break.
Note that there is some verbal material on the other side of the break—the Vice President's message. But it's only a fragment, and it doesn't make sense unless joined to the larger linguistic part on your computer. But that computer and yours are no longer linked, so from your vantage there appears to be no other linguistic material except the material you have on your computer. Likewise, your computer probably has some thumbnails of the spatial diagrams stored on it, but they're vague and undetailed. The detailed diagrams, which you'd normally access through the net, are stored somewhere else.

How much can we tell about the normal operation of an Internet connected computer by examining what it can do with the Internet connection cut? Not much, as it turns out. Once we cut that link, we've got a crippled machine, a machine that no longer is operating normally. And the same is true of your brain. Cut the corpus callosum, and you've severed two units that normally interchange information back and forth at will, thousands of times a second. There may be verbal abilities of various sorts in the right hemisphere, abilities that are tied across to the left and work smoothly with it as a unit. Cutting those links leaves isolated, useless fragments. You could easily conclude the right side of the brain was contributing nothing verbal at all, but you'd be mistaken. Likewise, the spatial processing may be done primarily in the right hemisphere, but it links smoothly to a lot of other spatial abilities that the left hemisphere helps out with. Cut the corpus callosum and these abilities may no longer be accessible because they were accessed across the corpus callosum. But it would be a mistake to assume that, therefore, they were never there.

That's where the left-brain/right-brain people go wrong. They look at the functioning of a brain with its critical intercommunication nexus severed, and assume that what the two now separate hemispheres can do reflects what they normally do. Yet normal brains never operate in this dichotomous fashion. The two halves of the brain work together even more flawlessly than your computer links to web sites that are actually stored on the other side of the world.

More recent research has suggested that the simple left-brain/right-brain split promoted by pop psychology is hopelessly simplistic. Eran Zaidel at UCLA, for example, has noted that both hemispheres of the brain become active when linguistic tasks are pursued (Benson & Zaidel, Eds., 1985). Elements of vocabulary, for example, are scattered around the brain to varying degrees.

Thus, it's almost impossible to wipe out all of someone's language with localized brain damage. Ironically, Paul Broca, the man whose research started it all, failed to notice that his original patient had suffered damage to more than just Broca's area. As we now realize, damage to just Broca's area alone would not have left his patient as profoundly unable to communicate.

The pop psychology view that mathematically or linguistically gifted individuals must be more "left-brained," as it turns out, is not supported by recent research at all. People who score highly on intelligence tests, and thus are highly gifted in language and math abilities, don't show any significant differences in left or right brain size or function. Recent studies of gifted individuals have discovered that the only significant difference between these people and their less adept peers is that the gifted individuals have corpus callosa that are significantly more extensive than those of average math and verbal ability (Luders, Bilder, Thompson, Szeszko, Hamilton, & Toga, 2007). These data suggests that there's a link between more integration of the hemispheres and math and verbal ability, rather than the naïve and simplistic explanation of domination of one hemisphere over the other.

Of course, we can't make any causal conclusions from correlational data – it's possible that being gifted makes the person create a bigger corpus callosum rather than the bigger corpus callosum making him or her gifted, and any number of other variables might be causing both a larger corpus collosum and giftedness. But what we don't see is any sign that simple hemispheric dominance plays a role in verbal, logic, or mathematical abilities, or in intuitive, spatial or artistic abilities and that's significant.

Old Brain vs. New Brain

I want to finish this chapter by looking at an example of a situation where some parts of the brain, while processing information about the world, actually come to substantially different conclusions from other parts, and then discussing how different people deal with this conflict. Here, we're going to look at a very important task for the brain – the process of recognizing familiar places, objects, and situations, evaluating them for possible dangers, and proposing particular actions that should occur should danger be present. Humans have two almost separate systems built into their brains that serve these purposes and that work in parallel with each other (Luria, 1973). One of those systems is evolutionarily old, being found in the most primitive of organisms with brains. The other is far more recent and much rarer in the animal kingdom. The first, and older of these motivational systems is centered in what is known as the limbic system. The limbic system, depicted in the diagram below, runs through the centers of both temporal lobes on either side of the brain, and then joins together through the top parts of the brain almost like the two halves of a wishbone join. (A look at the diagram below should make this more clear).

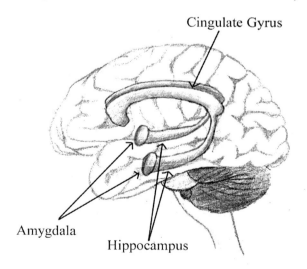

Cingulate Gyrus

Amygdala

Hippocampus

The critical part of this system for our current discussion are the two sections near the front, a pair of small sections known jointly as the amygdala

The amygdala is the central emotional processing section of the brain. When you're feeling emotional arousal, whether it be fear, surprise, anger, joy, or any of a myriad of other emotions, this section of the brain shows activity and appears to be responsible for the emotional feelings you experience. So we might call the amygdala the emotional center of the brain. The emotional center of the brain is fired up and driven into action when we experience sensory situations that resemble other emotion-inducing sensory situations we've experienced in the past. So if, for example, we run into a person who resembles somebody who has hurt us or frightened us in the past, fear will be aroused by the amygdala again when that person is seen or smelled or heard or felt, and we will be motivated by that fear to attempt to escape. If a location smells like, looks like, or in any other sensory mode reminds us of a location where we've had good experiences in the past, this new location will give rise to good feelings as well, and we will be motivated to remain in that location and relax. If a situation resembles a situation where we were made to feel guilty in the past, the new situation will arouse guilt, and we will be motivated to avoid that situation.

Let's say, for example, that you're an eighteen-month-old being taken to the doctor's office for a set of inoculations and booster shots. Now as a barely verbal tiny person, you don't understand much of the world, but you know when things hurt, and you're capable of seeing, hearing, smelling, feeling, and tasting. There you are in a white room, minding your own business, sitting snugly in Mom's or Dad's arms, smelling that medical antiseptic smell in the air, looking at the white walls, hearing the rustle of a starched uniform as the technician approaches. Suddenly, that person, possibly dressed in a distinctive color like white or aqua or plum, takes you firmly by the arm or leg *and then sticks a needle in you,* or *possibly several needles in succession!*

This is a most distressing turn of events, and you scream your little toddler head off, the pain of the needles driving you to struggle, ineffectually, to escape this assault on your person. At the same time, your brain associates certain things together. It takes in the setting and the people, including everything you saw, heard, smelled, tasted, and felt just prior to the sharp stabs of pain that caused you such fear and drove you to attempt to escape. Then it associates each of those sensory stimuli directly with that terrified emotional reaction. The visual memories are stored in your occipital lobes, the auditory and olfactory (smell) memories are stored in the temporal lobes, and the tactile (touch) memories are stored in the parietal lobes. But all of them are in turn connected, quite powerfully, to the fear and escape reaction via the amygdala. The assault on your person goes on long enough and is vivid enough to make those connections strong and powerful. Sure, you do escape, eventually, or at least they stop tormenting you. They even may give you a hug and a lollypop to suck on, and life gets toddler-good again and you go back to living in the moment as all the toddler set does.

Six months later, when you come in for your two-year checkup, they take you into that white room with its medical smells, and a person in the same white or aqua or plum outfit as before approaches. The brain matches the current sensory stimuli with stored memories, and all of those memories converge onto the amygdala, where they were associated with fear and pain due to your previous experience. As soon as that happens, your toddler brain begins screaming "Red alert! Red alert!" mental sirens go off, and you freak out, even if there or no needles and no shots in store for you this visit.

Now we're not talking about conscious memory here, we're talking about the quite unconscious connections to the equally unconscious amygdala. Conscious recall of past experiences is controlled and conducted elsewhere, in our impressive frontal lobes. These conscious memories can very well occur quite independently of any unconscious fear responses we might recall. In order to consciously remember having received shots from a person dressed in a particular way in a particular room in the past, we'd have to have stored away, in various parts of our brain, mental representations or images for each sensory impression. We'd have to have mental representations for the room, the person with the needle, the other objects in the room, and we'd have to pull those all together and then recreate the sequence of events in our frontal lobes, with our mental representations of each object being put in its proper place, and then the mental images of the actors moving through their paces as they happened in the real world. Visual images of each part of this memory would have to be retrieved from the occipital lobes, auditory memories from the temporal lobes, their spatial locations from the parietal lobes along with tactile images, and so on, and then they would have to be manipulated by those lobes in the time sequence that originally occurred. That's a tall order for a short person with only a couple of years' experience on the planet.

By contrast, the fear response can be fired up just by the new sights, sounds, smells, and touches matching mental representations that are tied directly to the emotional mechanism, a much simpler and less demanding task. It's no wonder, then, that you can have an emotional reaction to a stimulus without actually being able to fully or possibly even partially recall the stimulus situation from the past that triggered the reaction. To fear the doctor's office and the approaching health care worker, you only have to have a single link or two to the amygdala. But it takes more links, coordinated with each other, to consciously remember the past experience by assembling it with the frontal lobes. As a loud 2-year-old, you can feel intense fear when you re-enter the doctor's office without being able to consciously remember the original event that made you so fearful.

So we have two separate but linked recognition systems--conscious memories on one hand, and emotional reactions based on associations on the other. Conscious memories require us to recall enough of the original stimuli to recognize the past situation and make sense out of it, but emotional memories can function with far fewer associations that are far less clear. As a result, we'll have many situations where we feel emotional reactions even though we don't have enough original connections to remember why we feel that way. A particular setting makes us edgy, another one triggers anticipation of good things happening, and a third causes stark raving fear. You can feel that edginess, anticipation, or fear even if you can't consciously recall the original situation.

Thus, the ability to link emotions with outside stimuli appears early in humans. But ability to recall conscious memories is delayed. Sometime prior to age 4, your front lobes become capable of assembling memories of the past and setting them in time sequence, so that they can run almost like little movies in your head. Once this happens, the groundwork is laid for us to engage in one of the most important aspects of being a human – human reasoning. Reasoning takes the form of induction and deduction, and both depend upon conscious memories.

Induction is the process of extrapolating what is going to happen next by reviewing what has happened in this situation before, and then assuming that what has happened before is likely to happen the next time. Because this reviewing process requires memory for episodes, it's a frontal lobe function. Suppose we drop our favorite

Ming vase (and we all have a favorite Ming vase, I'm sure), and it shatters on the concrete floor. If we're trying to predict what would happen if we were to drop our formerly second-favorite Ming vase, now promoted to the status of new favorite, we dig though our memories and retrieve the memory of its predecessor's fate. We then predict that this new, somewhat lesser vase would probably meet the same fate as its predecessor were we to treat it just as carelessly. Likewise, if we heat water and it boils, we engage in induction by extrapolating to other heating devices on other days with other amounts of water, concluding that if we heat them, they will boil as well. That's induction, and it's based, obviously, on our past experiences and conscious memories.

The frontal lobes can also engage in deductive reasoning, which is a bit more complicated. A logician would tell you that deduction involves deriving the truths that are inherent in other truths using logical reasoning. To put it in simpler terms, deduction is often about how things are grouped together in the world. Logicians call groups of things "sets," and by knowing how one set is related to another, we can often then generate all sorts of relationships with still other sets. For example, if all dogs are of the genus canus and thus belong to that set, and Lutwidge is a dog, and thus belongs to the set dogs, then Lutwidge is of the genus canus, simply because the set of dogs is completely inside of the set "canus." Set logic is absolute – if an object is in set A, and set A is in set B, the object is also in set B.

"Give us a concrete example!" I hear you screaming. (Once again, I'm amazed at how far your voice carries. Especially as I can't hear half the stuff my wife says from 4 feet away. Have you considered becoming a professional announcer, or a hog caller?) One concrete example coming up. Let's say Sherlock Holmes is sawing away in a melancholy fashion on his violin (probably temporarily out of morphine and feeling down because of it), and

Dr. Watson is working on some medical paperwork (or trying to think of a colleague who might have some morphine he could get for Holmes so Holmes would stop that infernal sawing away on his violin). There's a knock on the door of 221B Baker Street, and Watson hurries to answer it (you don't expect a morphine junkie in withdrawal to answer the door, do you?). A man is standing there. Holmes takes one glance at him and says, "Quickly, Watson! Bring that man in! He's come all the way from Cornwall where he works as a potter to talk to us!"

The man's jaw drops, and he says, "I've never met you in my life, 'Olmes! 'Ow did you know I was a potter from Cornwall!"

And Holmes, of course, says, "Elementary, Watson!" (He doesn't say, "Elementary, my dear Watson," because at no point in Conan Doyle's original Sherlock Holmes stories does he utter that exact phrase. He does refer to "My dear Watson," and he says "Elementary, Watson" a lot, but he never quite strings the whole phrase together, even though it's become part of the popular Holmes mythology.) "Elementary, Watson!" Holmes says. "This man has calluses on his thumbs that are found only on potters! And he has a type of mud splashed all over his pant legs and boots that is found only in Cornwall! So obviously, he's a potter from Cornwall!"

Watson says, "Astounding, Holmes!" But it really isn't. It's simple deduction. The only thing that's astounding is that Holmes collects idle trivia in his memory such as what types of calluses are found on every type of working person, and what kind of mud is found in every insignificant crevice of the United Kingdom. Once you have those facts, the rest of the exercise is simple deduction that even a 10-year-old could do. If only potters have those types of calluses, and your man has those types of calluses, he must be a potter, because we've established that the set of people with those sorts of calluses is completely enclosed by the set of people who are potters. If that type of mud is only found in Cornwall, and he has that type of mud on his pants, his pants, at least, have recently been in Cornwall. It's simple deduction.

Unfortunately, there's a weakness to deduction that keeps it from being the ultimate solution to all human problems. It relies utterly on the premises of the argument being absolutely true. If one of your premises is false, we're left in limbo. What if there are other ways of getting calluses such as those found on our hypothetical visitor to Holmes? What if, for example, operators of hansom cabs also get them from holding the reins? Well, then, all bets are off, and we have no way of knowing if the man is a potter or not. If mud just like that on our purported potter's pants is found in Soho, Gloucester, and along the banks of the Mersey, then Holmes' deductions are also brought into question. Only if his original, remembered premises are true, can he say he's proven his conclusions.

But both induction and deduction are based on past memories, conscious memories retrieved by the front lobes and used as a basis of our reasoning. Let's say, for example, you've got the goods on Lutwidge, the shady accountant at work. When anticipating what Lutwidge might do when you confront him, you could use induction. You might reason, "When I've cornered animals in the past and they've been frightened, they've sometimes lashed out at me. And when people are cornered on TV shows, they also lash out. Lutwidge is backed into a corner, and there doesn't appear to be any chance he can escape charges of embezzlement. He is fairly likely, therefore, to lash out, so we'd all better watch ourselves when we confront him." This particular conclusion of yours is based on cold calculation, rather than the hot emotions that the amygdala deals out. You can readily explain to other people why you're expecting trouble from Lutwidge, and back it up with evidence from your past experiences in the form of retrieved memories.

Now it's possible that your emotion-based processor will also evaluate this situation and come to a similar conclusion. Elements of it may match fearful situations in the past – the fear of Lutwidge's face when you confront him, the furtive, rapid flicking of his eyes, the twitching of his muscles, the sidelong glances toward the door—all might match the movements of that feral cat you thought you were going to trap when you were eight, the one that flew at your face moments later (with quite disturbing results). These similarities in the current situation may activate your emotional response system in your amygdala and arouse a fear response similar to the one caused by that cat many years ago. Even more interesting, it can arouse that fear without you consciously tapping the declarative memory of the long ago cat attack, so you might find yourself feeling edgy and feel your fear rising without knowing why you have that fear. Later, after Lutwidge has vaulted past you and fled, you might tell people, "I had a hunch he was going to run just before he bolted, but by then it was too late."

Hunches, also known as intuition, are probably simply elements of memory that we can't consciously retrieve, including emotional responses of the amygdala. The associations are there, we can't remember where they came from, so we call them intuitions. But they're no different from the memories we can consciously retrieve, they're just so incomplete that we can't consciously retrieve the whole memory and pinpoint the original source of our feelings.

So we can fire up emotional responses without being able to consciously recall the scenario where we learned the responses. That means that there is the potential for our conscious reasoning to come to one conclusion, while at the same time the emotional system is signaling another one. Let's go back to you as an adorable toddler (and you were adorable, make no mistake about it. Heck, you're still adorable now). You might not consciously remember having been so rudely poked full of holes during your last doctor visit. But the fear associations that the emotional processing system formed might remain. Your mother decides it's time to take a lovely picture of her adorable toddler, and takes you to the photo studio, which just happens to be a small, white room with a table on one side just about the height of the examination table in the doctor's office. Your dear mother carries you into the room, sits in a chair by the table, and suddenly a person in a plum or aqua or white outfit approaches with a big smile, holding something in her hand (it happens to be a shutter trigger, not a needle, but you're 2, remember?). "Mayday! Mayday! Mayday!" goes the amygdala, you freak out, and the relatives are just going to have to take her word for it for a while longer concerning how adorable you are, because there certainly aren't going to be any precious wallet-sized keepsakes produced today.

This sometimes disconnect between these two connected systems of the brain doesn't end with the rise of coherent memories and the ability to reason, though. Let's consider a slightly older child— perhaps an older brother, a sturdy, no-nonsense, relatively brave little explorer. Roaming in his own back yard one day, he finds that a board in the fence is loose. In fact, the board is so loose that he can force it aside, making a hole in the bottom of the fence big enough he can put his freckled face in there. So he does, and squats down and he peers into the neighbor's yard, a kingdom that he has never seen before. Just as he gets settled down low enough to see, the neighbor's St. Bernard, who had been watching the board move with a fascination of his own, bounds forward, lowers his huge snout to the ground and the newly opened hole, plants both paws framing the face just on the other side of the boards, and erupts with a thunderous "Woof! Woof! Woofwoofwoof!"

Now this huge dog doesn't have a ghost of a chance of fitting through this small hole under the fence, and he's full of exuberant cheer and rollicking good fun, not menace, but that doesn't really register in our intrepid explorer. After a backwards flying summersault to his feet that that would have done a Cirque du Soleil performer proud followed by a hasty retreat into the house, our little guy finally puts enough doors between him and his exuberant new acquaintance that he can stop running in terror and try to start breathing again. But this frightening experience has already left a mark deeper than somewhat damp trousers. The very sight of a broad, furry dog face, a waggling tail or the sound of a bark has made its impression on the emotional response system, the net result being that now our little guy is uncontrollably afraid of dogs.

So what's different here? Unlike his younger sister, he can consciously remember the cause of his fear, namely, his encounter with the neighbor's oversized pooch. So both his ancient emotional memory system and his much more evolutionarily modern conscious memory system agree that dogs aren't exactly the cat's pajamas, and he reacts with fear and a desire for a quick escape when the family runs across one in the future.

But you can't escape dogs, and the family has many friends and relatives who have them. The parents find having a shaking, cowering, 50 pound lump in their arms or laps every time a dog pokes its head into the room extremely inconvenient. So naturally they appeal to reason. They drag to boy over to friendly dogs and pet them while crooning to the shaking child, "Look, he's a nice doggy. He won't hurt you. Come on, pet the doggy."

The thing is, we're talking about two connected, but independently operating memory systems here. Even if you convince the child, intellectually, that this dog and many other dogs won't hurt him, his amygdala and his emotional memory system are screaming "Run away! Run away!" louder than Sir Robin when pursued by Frenchmen. He might pet the dog, because you're making him, but he'll still shake like a leaf in a brisk breeze during the process. It's also likely that his emotional memory system will shriek the same fear warnings to him the next time he sees a dog or a dog-like animal even after having gotten along well with this one. His conscious mind can retrieve all sorts of memories of pleasant, calm dogs, but that won't stop his emotional system from reacting. One part of his brain is saying, "There's no need to fear," and the other part is screaming, "Abort! Eject! Abandon ship!"

There are obviously tremendous advantages to having two systems monitoring our situation at all times and ready to motivate us into action. With two systems, we can recognize a wider range of situations that might work to our advantage or that might threaten us than we'd be able to recognize with only one. But there is a disadvantage of having two different interlocking systems, too. You have to be able to deal with the situation where your systems conflict-- situations where one system is telling you to approach, whereas the other system is telling you to run for your life. In that situation, the emotional system often holds sway, and we may not be motivated by logical argument at all. My dear old mother, for example, made it clear years ago that she had no intention of setting foot in an airplane under any conditions. When I tried to argue with her that she would be considerably safer flying across the country than riding the same distance in a car with my father (an excellent driver for his age, but that's no protection from the people he shares the road with, and even excellent drivers get fatigued and make mistakes), my mother cut me short by stating that it was no point in trying to reason with her, because she already knew, intellectually, that commercial airplanes were much safer than any other means of transportation. That knowledge didn't help, though – her emotional system was never going to let her set foot on an airplane.

We often encounter situations where our conscious, reasoning, logical mind is telling us one thing, but our gut reactions, our feelings, are telling us another. A large number of factors probably play a role in which module of our mind will determine our behavior when they are in conflict like this. People vary in the degree to which they become emotionally aroused, and they vary in their abilities to use inductive and deductive logic. The net result is, some people will probably be driven or motivated mostly by their emotions, whereas other people will be driven or motivated mostly by their reasoning. Emotional motivation is especially likely if the person just isn't that good at inductive or deductive logic. As any campaign manager will tell you, you don't have to convince them, you just have to scare them. This is why fear-mongering is such an excellent campaign technique.

Our brains consist of many different parts, all with their own individual but interlocking functions. It's all in use, although it's not all in use simultaneously. Being logical or artistic isn't a matter of being left-brained or right-brained, it's a matter of how the entire unit works together. Because this complex structure consists of many parts, there will be times when one part of our brains is counseling one course of action, while other part is counseling another, perhaps contradictory course of action instead.

In truth, we treat our brains badly. We smash beer cans against our heads, bounce soccer balls off them, and several times a year (at least in my case) give them a good, sharp crack against a cabinet door or some other unseen obstruction. Yet this crazy, beautiful, wonderful, insanely complicated structure that we've got taking up the bulk of the space inside our heads, operates surprisingly coherently most of the time, even though our thoughts are sometimes contradictory, scrambled, or leave us at odds with ourselves. You're not intuitive or rational, left-brained or right-brained. You're just brained. Frankly, I have always found that sufficient for my needs.

References:

Benson, F., & Zaidel, Eran (Eds.) (1985). The dual brain: Hemispheric specialization in humans. New York: Guilford Press.

Eggert, G. H. (1977). Wernicke's works on aphasia: A sourcebook and review (janua linguarum). Berlin: Walter de Gruyter

Erdmann, E., & Stover, D. (2000). *Beyond a World Divided: Human Values in the Brain-Mind Science of Roger Sperry.* Lincoln, Nebraska: iUniverse.

Giedd, J. N., Blumenthal, J., Jeffries, N.O., Castellanos, F. X., Liu, H., Zijdenbos, A, et al. (1999). Brain Development during childhood and adolescence: A longitudinal MRI study. *Nature Neuroscience, 2(10)*, 861-863.

Luders, E., Narr, K. L., Bilder, R. M., Thompson, P. M., Szeszko, P. R., Hamilton, L., & Toga, A. W. (2007). Positive correlations between corpus callosum thickness and inteligence. *Neuroimage, 37(4),* 1457-1464.

Luria, A. R. (1973). *Working Brain: An Introduction to Neuropsychology.* New York: Basic Books.

Schiller, F. (1992). *Paul Broca: Founder of French Anthropology, Explorer of the Brain.* Oxford: Oxford University Press.

Williams, L. V. (1986). *Teaching for the 2-sided mind: A guide to right-brain, left-brain education.* New York: Simon and Schuster.

Chapter 6: Averages, Variance, and Why the English Language Sucks

"There are three kinds of lies: lies, damned lies and statistics." (Quote attributed by Mark Twain in his autobiography to Benjamin Disraeli but almost certainly from some earlier source.)

"Statistics are no substitute for judgment." (American orator Henry Clay)

"I abhor averages. I like the individual case. A man may have six meals one day and none the next, making an average of three meals per day, but that is not a good way to live." (Supreme Court Justice Louis D. Brandeis

"Welcome to Lake Wobegon, where all the women are strong, all the men are good-looking, and all the children are above average." (Garrison Keillor, introduction to his *A Prairie Home Companion*)

The Lure of Averages

Statistics are a critical indicator of many of the most important things we need to know about the world. We need to know when illness rates are rising, when climates are changing, when sales are plummeting, and when the cost of prescription drugs is skyrocketing. Without statistics many things in the world would change subtly without our knowledge, and by the time they changed enough for us to notice, it might be too late to act to prevent catastrophe. We need statistics, and we use them daily to our advantage.

The most widely cited statistics are often averages. How often do we hear averages in news reports, in political debates, and in discussions of public policy? We worry about average income, average weight and height of adults and children, and average scores on standardized tests. Every financial report starts with the Dow Jones Industrial Average, applicants to college worry about the average SAT scores of other applicants, and most students in general are worried about the most crucial statistic of them all, their grade point averages. Averages give us a simple, clear way to grasp incomprehensibly larger groups of numbers (and most of the time, for most of us, more than about 7 numbers is an incomprehensibly large group). Averages give us the impression that we have some idea what's going on with those numbers. They may even convince us we totally understand the numbers. It's that danger I want to warn you against in this chapter, because averages have the potential to be the most misleading numbers on Earth.

Averages are measures of central tendency, or the value around which everything centers. Although we talk about "the" average, in fact what we consider the average may be any one of three different things – the mean, the mode, or the median. The mean is a mathematical construction that is created by adding up all the values in a group and then dividing that total by the number of values. The mode is the value that appears more often in the group than any other. The median is the value that is found exactly in the center of the group when the values are placed in order. For illustration, let us consider a family with 7 children of differing ages. The couple has a 2 year-old, a set of 4-year-old twins, a nine-year-old, a 10-year-old, a 12-year-old, and a 15-year-old. What is the average age of their children? The mean age of the children would be obtained by adding all the ages together and dividing by the total number of children. Added together, the total of the children's ages is 2 + 4 + 4 + 9 + 10 + 12 + 15, or 56. The total number of children is 7, so dividing the total of the ages by 7 gives us a mean of 8. But the mode, or most common value, is 4. And the median, or the value in the middle, is 9, because when we put the ages in order, 3 of the children are younger than 9, and three are older.

So which of these is the average age of children in the family, four, eight, or nine? Technically, they all are, because each of them, the mode, the mean, and the median, are measures of central tendency. Yet, none of them describes the family very well. Only 2 of the people in the family actually are 4, the mode, only one is 9, the median, and none of the children in the family at all are the mean age of 8. Suppose we want to buy a video game for the children to play, and we want to get a game the average child in the family can play. No matter which average we use, the game probably will satisfy only a few family members.
So the average gives us the illusion of grasping the ages of the children in the family, but in fact does nothing of the sort. Two of the averages describe only a tiny portion of the group, and one describes no people in the group at all. This tendency to be representative of few group members is often the case with averages. As statistics professors are fond of pointing out, the average American has one ovary, one testicle, and half a uterus. (In this case, the average the professors are using is the mean. But if you had one ovary, one testicle, and half a uterus, you'd probably be mean, too).

I run into this problem of averages misleading people all the time in my Adolescent Psychology and Psychology of Parenting classes, when students ask me when the average boy or girl enters puberty, possibly with a wary eye toward when their own sweet little boy or girl will officially become that most dreaded of juvenile forms, an adolescent. The textbooks will tell you that the average girl enters puberty at age 10, and the average boy enters puberty at age 12. So now you know what to expect of your children, right?

Except that only a tiny minority of girls enter puberty right at the age of 10, or even close to that age. Fully half of girls will enter puberty after that age, because the average we're talking about here is the median, or the middle of the group. The other half will already have entered puberty by the age of 10, some of them substantially earlier than 10. The actual variation from that median number is rather astounding. Girls can enter puberty as early as 7 ½ or as late as 14 and still be within the range of normalcy. Boys can enter puberty as early as 9 or as late as 17 and still be within the range of normalcy (Ge, et al., (2007). The variation in age of entering puberty for both sexes is so broad that neither the means, nor the medians, nor the modes describe very many of the people in either the boys' or the girls' distributions. And because these averages don't describe many of the people in the distribution, they aren't very useful at all to our anxious parents in determining when their children will enter puberty.

Means, modes, and medians become much more useful when values of a variable cluster tightly around some central number. If the children in the family we talked about above consisted of a set of 7-year-old twins, a set of 8-year-old triplets , and a set of 9-year-old twins, our mean would be 8, our median would be 8, and our mode would be 8. All these averages would be a fairly good description of the children in the family, and a video game bought for the average child would probably keep them all entranced no matter which average we used. Such a tight distribution is rare, though --most of the really useful things we wish to understand don't cluster like that—they spread across a wide range of values.

There's an official name for the amount of spreading of a distribution of values. That spreading tendency is called the variance. If the numbers in a distribution cover a wide range, then we say the variance of the distribution is high. If they span only a very narrow range, we say the variance is low. When the variance is low, averages give us a good grasp of a large number of the members of the group. But when variance is high, as is the case with the age of onset of puberty, the average, whether it's the mean, the mode, or the median, can be downright misleading.

Then, there's a second problem that can make averages misleading. Sometimes a set of numbers is arranged symmetrically around the mean and the median, so that there are about as many low numbers and high numbers, and both the low numbers and the high numbers are about the same distance from the mean or median. But sometimes such a set of numbers is asymmetrical. When a distribution of numbers is asymmetrical, the mean, especially, is often highly misleading. For example, you might have fewer low than high numbers, but the low numbers are farther from the median. Say we have a family with a 1-year-old, a 15-year-old, a pair of 16-year-old twins, and an 18-year-old. Again, you want to buy a video game for the family that most of the children will enjoy. The median age of this group is 16, and that number also describes the group fairly well, with the exception of one child. But the mean is only 11, a number that really doesn't describe anyone in the group. Buy a present that matches the median, and you're much more likely the favorite aunt or uncle than if you buy one that matches the mean. Asymmetrical distributions like this make the mean a much less useful statistic.

A good example of such an asymmetrical distribution is the distribution of family income in a country such as the United States. Most of the families in the United States are in the low to middle income ranges. Only a much smaller number make high and very high family incomes. But because some of the small number who make high incomes make very high incomes indeed, the distribution is highly asymmetrical. I can illustrate this on a smaller scale if we consider a group of families all connected to the Lutwidge soap manufacturing company in one way or another. The parents in Family A are part-time janitors for the factory, and between them make $24,000 a year. The parent in Family B is a single mom who works the production floor watching label printers, and makes $26,000 a year. The parent in Family C is her supervisor, and makes $29,000 a year. In Family D the father is unemployed and the mother works as a clerk for the company, making $33,000 a year. Family E's sole worker is a middle manager, making 70,000 a year, as is the case with Family F. Family G has a part time worker and a full time worker in it, both working the sales office and making $76,000 a year between them. Family H, which includes a high level manager, makes $650,000 a year. And Family I, wealthy stockholders in that company, make $750,000 a year. So what is the average family income for this group?

The median income in this example is the income of the family in the middle of the distribution, Family E, which is $70,000 a year. That, by itself, is misleading enough. After all, a lot of the people who make less than this make considerably less – in fact, every family making less makes less than half as much, so this number doesn't describe those people well at all. But, because the distribution is highly asymmetrical, the mean is even more misleading – the mean, in this case, is $200,000 a year! Now let us suppose that the company's board of directors decides to raise company productivity and become, "lean and mean" in order to boost the company's stock price. So a new CFO is brought in who immediately gives all the production staff a pay cut approximately 20% (with minor variations here and there) and thus slightly lowers the product cost to undercut the competition. As a result of this, the company stock rises sharply, because product sales go up and raise income of the company, but costs go down. What effect is had on the people who work for it? The following year, Family A makes $20,000 a year. The parent in Family B, still doing the same job watching the label printers, makes $23,000 a year. The parent in Family C has to make do with only $24,000 that year. In Family D the father remains unemployed and the mother's clerk salary is lowered to $27,000 a year. Our Family E's middle manager keeps his 70,000 a year salary. Family F's manager gets a $15,000 bonus for laying off the entire full time technical repairs staff and making his workers do computer repair in addition to their other duties. Sales works on commission, and the new lower prices of the product send sales up, so Family G's sales people make a big income gain, making $101,000 in this next year. Family H, with the high level manager, makes $650,000 a year, plus the breadwinner gets an $100,000 bonus for having raised company productivity. And Family I, the wealthy stockholders, get big dividends plus stock incentives that raise their income to $1.6 million.

So now what are the median and mean incomes? Many of the people in our example are suffering with much less income than before. Yet you can't see that in the statistics: our median income is still $70,000, and our mean is up by 50%, to a whopping $300,000 a year!

That actually is something like what has been happening in the United States for many years, with only minor year to year variations. Overall median income has remained about the same or shown modest increases from one year to the next (with the rare modest decrease here and there). Yet, at the same time, a lot of families feel they are much worse off, especially those on the lower end of the income scale. And they're absolutely right, regardless of what the averages say. Because although the averages are rising, net wages for most workers actually fell at the same time.

If we were to talk about mean income, one would get a very false picture of the prosperity of the average household, but obviously the mean is not the statistic to use here. In a skewed distribution, the mean doesn't represent the typical American at all. But the median is only marginally better than the mean, because the variance is very high, and thus the range of incomes is vast. Let's consider, therefore, the statistics on the income of households in America. Not only is the range of incomes wide, making averages not a good description of the group, but they keep getting progressively wider. You can see this if you look at the differences in income of the richest and poorest households in the United States. According to the Census Bureau, in 1980, the poorest 20% of the population had a household median income of $4,483, and the wealthiest 20% a household median of $46,053 (www.census.gov, 2010). So the wealthiest 20% of the population made a little more than 10 times as much as the poorest 20%. By the year 2000, the median household income of the poorest 20% of the population was $10,157, and the median household income of the wealthiest 20% was $142,269, or 14 times the income of the poorest 1/5. In the words of my dear old mother, the rich got richer, and the poor got poorer.

The effect is even greater if we compare the bottom 20% of households to the wealthiest 5%. The wealthiest 5% of households had a median income of $66,617 in 1980, or almost 15 times that of the poorest 20%. But by 2000, the wealthiest 5% of households had a median income of $252,400, or 25 times higher than that of the poorest 20% of households.

All of which means that the variance or range in household incomes in the United States is very large, and that variance has been getting progressive larger. Just as was the case for our family age examples above, as variance increases, the ability of averages like the median to describe the population decreases proportionately. As a result, the median income of American households describes fewer and fewer people all the time. So when the Census Bureau reported in 2007 that the median income had risen, and that the median household in the United States had an income of $50,233, you have to bear in mind that this number describes the experience of very few American households, and that those who make less often make far, far less. Indeed, an increase in income of the wealthiest Americans alone, or a decrease in income among the poorest, would still leave the median unchanged, and if both things happened, mean income might rise even when income for a majority of people was dropping. Such a shift would appear as a change in the variance, but variance changes are almost never reported, only "averages."

Math Scores

So what does this have to do with the price of liver on a stick, or of tea in China? Quite a lot, actually, if we're talking about mean or median prices, and whether you'll be able to buy a cup of tea for the mean or the median price rather than paying substantially more or less in the particular tea house where you're sitting at the moment. But, putting that aside, it has quite a lot to do with an issue involving China, Japan, and often Korea as well. In this case, I'm talking about the use of average performance on standardized tests as an indicator of the performance of educational establishments in Far Eastern countries compared to the performance of American educational establishments.

Every year Americans are bombarded with statistics suggesting that our children are performing poorly in fundamental intellectual abilities such as math or reading. These statistics usually involve mean or median scores in standardized tests of reading comprehension or calculation. For example, in 2004 the Program for International Assessment (PISA) reported that children from the US ranked 24th out of 29 industrialized countries in math skill, with Singapore taking the top spot. Our rank among these industrialized countries does, by itself, sound ominous, and newspapers across the US reveled in trumpeting that it was another sign of doom for Americans and a sure sign the Apocalypse, Armageddon, and the end of life as we know are all near. The Wall Street Journal headline read, "Economic Time Bomb: U.S. Teens Are Among Worst at Math" in bold type (Wall Street Journal, 2004). Commentators shook their heads, cited the evils of the public school system, teachers' unions, uncaring parents, greedy corporations, or incompetent politicians, depending on their political cant, and all preached gloom and doom. Everyday Americans took it as yet another sign that the world was going to Hell in a hand basket.

But are American teens really worse when it comes to math than the teens in Singapore, or Japan, or even Poland? Is our math performance substandard, inevitably driving us down into some sort of intellectual backwater? Will the major discoveries in math and science and the innovation those discoveries drive move to other countries? Are all our kids just less bright at math?
No one honestly knows, when you get right down to it, at least not from statistics like these. Remember, if a population has much variance, means, modes, and medians don't describe very many of the individuals in it. So what about the variances of these scores? Do the means really mean anything? Are the variances in these different countries comparable?

That's where the picture gets a lot more complicated very quickly. It turns out that variances in math scores on standardized tests are pretty darn large in all countries, and that the variance of standardized math scores is much higher in the US than in countries in the Far East. So the means and medians themselves don't describe many students, and differences in the variances make those averages tough to compare, anyway (No Country Left Behind, 2010).

The higher variance of scores of Americans doesn't mean that all American children are performing lower than children of these other countries. In industrialized countries in general, the top-performing children tend to perform fairly comparably—in other words, our best are roughly the same as their best. The bulk of the difference in mean performance is that the worst American students are much, much worse than the worst students in those other countries. The variance of scores in Japan and China and Singapore and even Poland are all much narrower, mostly because the lowest performing students don't go to quite the depths of ineptitude that our lowest performing students reach.

One can come up with all sorts of reasons why this is so – we're an individualistic culture, not a collectivist one, so we focus more on individual performance than the performance of the group. That drives the highest performers to do their best, but discourages the lowest performers. You might also note that the poverty gap is much wider in the US than in those other countries, as we discussed above, so the rich are much richer and the poor much poorer in the US. The gap in quality of schools is also much wider mainly because of the poverty gap, so the best schools in the US are among the best in the world, but quality of schools dips much, much lower when we go to the worst schools. And parental and student attitudes toward the value of math vary much more in American culture. Most Japanese parents, for example, believe that math skill is one of the major keys to success in life, and they respond to this belief by beginning the training of their kids in math at about the same time they begin potty training. But attitudes toward math skill are much more variable in the US, where you will even find substantial minorities of parents who believe that most people don't need any math at all beyond counting, adding, subtracting, and multiplying (with even long division considered iffy in their minds). Asian parents are thus more uniformly behind the importance of learning math than their American counterparts (meaning variance in pressure to do well at math is larger in the US). (Park and Briel, 1998)

Does a lower average score mean American scientists and mathematicians are in danger of being eclipsed by their more thoroughly prepared competitors in other countries? Probably not. What Lyndon Johnson called the "best and the brightest" of American students are probably as good as any students in the world, and perform comparably. And it's that group who'll actually be competing on the world stage, not the lower performing end of the population. But that lower performing end of the population pulls American medians and means down, giving a confusing picture of the true state of the population. By focusing only on the "average," and not considering the variance of the populations, we reach a conclusion that the entire group of American children perform less well from one end of the distribution to the other, and we suggest a uniformity in performance not reflected in the data.

This is not to say that it's okay that we do such a poor job of educating our poorest performing students in the basics of mathematics. It's a crying shame that this happens, and few people honestly care. As educators, my colleagues and I haven't done enough to convince the average American that it's essential that his or her child learn math to the best of his or her ability, and it's also essential that everyone else's kids do so. (Personally, I want the kids who will be running the country when I'm old to know math well enough that they can keep things going, continue to advance technology, and understand public and private finance). But averages like the mean and median may falsely give the impression that all American children and adults, even the brightest, perform less well than teens in comparable countries, yet they really tell us nothing about that question.

Comparing Apples and Grapefruit

Averages are also misleading when the things you're comparing aren't all that comparable. If I were to tell you that the average grapefruit has a greater circumference and weighs more than the average apple, would you therefore conclude that the grapefruit is superior to the apple? Of course, not, not in a million years. Grapefruit are horrible, vile things that I wouldn't miss if they were wiped off the face of the Earth and wouldn't wish as a breakfast staple on my worst enemy, whereas apples are darned tasty. Sure, they're not entirely different things, they're both fruits. But they're different enough that things like size comparisons are meaningless. You'd also never conclude the grapefruit farmer is a better farmer than the apple farmer because he grows larger fruits. Yet when we compare average performances of American students to the average performances of children counting and spelling in other countries, we're doing exactly that.

For example, 5-year-old Taiwanese children can count much higher, on the average, than American children of the same age (Miller, et al., 1995). Is this more evidence of our failing education system? Not exactly. For one thing, we're dealing with children here who have not yet started formal schooling, so we can't really blame the schools for this one. Are the parents at fault for this difference, then? Maybe. But then again, maybe we're comparing apples to grapefruit.

How can that be? I hear you cry. Don't people worldwide use the same Arabic numbering system. Yes, that much is true. The numbering system and symbols are the same, but not the number names. We're comparing applies to grapefruit, because Taiwanese children count in Mandarin Chinese, but American children count *in English*. And when it comes to counting, as well as performing a number of other intellectual tasks, one can only conclude that English sucks.

"How dare you!" I hear you cry. "English is one of the most widely used languages in the world. It's the official world language of science, of diplomacy, and of air traffic control (really!). How can you attack this fine bastion of oral tradition by using such a disgusting gutter phrase from that same fine oral tradition?" Hey, don't get me wrong, I love English – it's the only language I actually can speak intelligibly (how intelligibly, you can judge for yourself from this narrative). But English is kind of like a 1963 Corvette Stingray split window coupe. It's flashy and fun, and it gets the job done in fine style. But it's quirky, not easily handled by everyone, and those beautiful split windows leak in the rain.

Languages, numbering systems, and other inventions of groups of humans that make us more intellectually capable are known by cognitive psychologists as "tools of intellectual adaptation." Like tools we use for physical tasks, they're creations of humans that are then passed on to other humans, and thus enhance our functionality and ability to survive. Other tools of intellectual adaptation include abaci, the Dewey Decimal System, digital computers, search engines, and Spam. (Just kidding about the Spam. By now you've probably noticed that Monty Python is forever branded upon my consciousness).

All languages are tools of intellectual adaptation, but not all languages are equally good tools. To enable communication of ideas, a language has to be complex enough to communicate sophisticated, abstract ideas, yet simple enough to learn and to teach to others, especially our children. All languages currently in use are rich and full and functional. But some languages lend themselves to use more easily than others.

English has some advantages – it has a lot of words, so it covers a lot of situations and is useful in a lot of contexts, and it largely avoids some complicated, unnecessary frills like gender (more about that later). But the basic numbers in English are unnecessarily complicated, considerably more complicated than the basic numbers in Mandarin Chinese. To count to 100 in English, you have to memorize the numbers from one through thirteen, all of which are different from the previous numbers. The number fourteen is a combination of a previous number, four, and the suffix "teen," but then comes fifteen, which is not "five" and "teen" but is altered to the easier to say "fifteen," as a result of cognitive economizing (an issue discussed Chapter 2). Then English falls into a regular pattern with "sixteen," "seventeen," "eighteen," and "nineteen." But after that, you have to learn a new term, "twenty."

English counting then settles into a sensible pattern for awhile, just using the original 9 numbers with the prefix "twenty," but when you get to "twenty-nine," you have to learn a new term again, "thirty." You can then combine that term with the numbers one through nine again until you get to forty, which sounds like the number four with the suffix "ty" added. And that's a pattern that repeats with "sixty, seventy, eighty, and ninety" when you get to them. But first, you have to learn the irregular new form, "fifty," which isn't "fivety," again for no particular reason other than that that's what everyone does.

Now contrast that with learning to count in Mandarin Chinese. Again you have to learn the words for the numbers one through ten. But thereafter, the numbers fall into a predictable, regular pattern. "Eleven," referred to by a new and different word in English, is "ten-one" in Mandarin. "Twelve" is "ten-two," and so on through the teens. When you get to twenty, you don't need a new term -- "twenty" is "two-ten," and twenty-one is "two-ten-one," and so on. This pattern continues on without alteration throughout the two-digit series. You don't have to learn another new counting word in Mandarin Chinese until you get to 100, and after that you don't need another new word until you get to 10,000! Is it any wonder preschoolers and kindergartners in Taiwan can count higher, on the average, than American children of the same age? It's a different task for them to learn, a considerably easier task, because you don't have to memorize so many new terms when you're learning in Mandarin Chinese. The difference in average counting ability of 5-year-olds means less than it appears, because we're comparing a group of children counting in a simpler system to a group of children counting in a more complex one. In other words, we're comparing apples to grapefruits.

So why don't we change English to make counting easier to learn? It wouldn't be that hard, after all? Well, consider this. I'm typing, at this very moment, on what is commonly called a "qwerty" keyboard—a design invented by Christopher Sholes in 1874 for the Remington typewriter company. The qwerty keyboard was named for the pseudo-word spelled by the first 5 letters on the top row of the keys, when read from the left. It was originally designed to prevent keys from clashing with each other in early typewriters. That was a real problem, especially for fast typists, because the keys all had to converge onto the very same spot on the platen in order for the letters to all be in a neat line. But that meant that the key for the next letter you were typing had some probability of coming in behind the previous key soon enough to strike the back of it and cause a key jam. To keep that from happening, Sholes put commonly-used keys in non-optimal positions to slow typing down, and he put keys that were commonly used in succession where they would have to be used by the same finger, or where the key would be far from the one commonly paired with it. The net result was that many of the more commonly used letters aren't in optimal positions. "E," and "T," the two most commonly used letters, are on the top row and require one to move fingers up from the normal typing position to strike them. "A," another common key, is under the left little finger, generally the weakest, least capable finger for most right handed folks. "O," "N" and "I" are also off the main row. Letters that are commonly pressed in succession to spell words, such as "ed," or "rt" actually have to be pressed by the same finger, which takes longer that typing them with two different fingers, but guarantees they'll never be pressed fast enough in succession to jam.

Now contrast that with a much better-designed alternative to the qwerty keyboard. The Dvorak keyboard puts the letters "A," "O," "E," and "U" directly under the fingers of the left hand, and "H," "T," "N," and "S" under the fingers of the right hand. The two most common letters in the English language, "E" and "T," are directly under your longest, strongest fingers. Studies have demonstrated unequivocally that people trained on the Dvorak keyboard learn quicker, make fewer errors, and type faster than those using the qwerty keyboard. So why is this abomination of nineteenth century engineering still in widespread use?
The answer is the same as the answer to why we don't improve the counting system in English. All the people who know the old system, which is practically everyone, would have to learn the new one, and they'd find it having to do so uncomfortable. (Actually, they'd scream at the top of their lungs about it. If you're old

enough, you'll remember what happened in the 1970's when America attempted to shift to the metric system). The fact that new people learning to type or learning to count have problems doesn't concern those of us who've already learned—we've already gone through it and survived. That creates a kind of linguistic inertia, with the majority of people willing to keep things just as they are and resisting movement.

It isn't just in our number names that English makes things unnecessarily complex compared to some other languages, and muddies comparisons of average intellectual performances of children in different cultures. We've already talked about 'rithmetic, so let's move on to the other two of the "three R's," readin' and 'ritin'.

Let us suppose that we want to compare basic reading and writing abilities in different countries. We've got the same problem we had before, that means and medians don't necessarily capture the experience of the average child well, especially if the variances of abilities in the two countries are different. We've also got the problem that we're comparing children trying to do a job using different tools, tools that may differ in capabilities. It's the latter issue we want to focus on here. Can we compare average reading and writing abilities of children in two cultures if they're using different tools of intellectual adaptation?

Consider this: If we were asked compare how quickly American children can look up the meaning of words using a digital computer with a high speed Internet connection to how well children from rural South Africa can look up the same words using a physical dictionary, we'd probably protest that our study was a waste of time, and the comparison wasn't fair to the rural South African children, who are using a less good tool of intellectual adaption. Dictionaries are good, and fun (see chapter 2), and they have their place, but computers are faster and have access to more comprehensive information. Yet the same thing happens when we compare average literacy rates in the U. S. with literacy rates in countries where different languages are spoken. Because again, we're comparing average apples to average grapefruits. Compared to many languages, when it comes to ease of learning to read and ease of learning to spell, English sucks.

I'm not saying that English doesn't have lots of words – it does, more than a million when you consider proper names and specialized vocabularies and obscure words used by just a few people. It isn't that English can't communicate complex ideas either – in the hands of a master, it does that superbly. It's just that English often accomplishes its communication in unnecessarily complex ways, ways that are simpler in some other languages. We'll begin with the real Achilles' heel of written English, spelling. To read and write in English, one has to be able to spell things in English. And English spelling is ridiculously, ludicrously, and unnecessarily complex. Rather than having one sound per letter and one letter per sound as some other languages do, in English there are letters that make more than one sound, and sounds that are represented by more than one letter. The letter "c" can make two different sounds, for example, an "s" sound in words like "cease" and a "k" sound in words like "cake." The letter "g" sometimes makes its own sound, as in the word "golf" and sometimes sounds like "j," as in "gesture." The vowels each make multiple sounds, depending on what letters follow them. The letter "e" sounds one way if an "a" follows it or a consonant and then a vowel, (each, elaborate), but makes another sound if two consonants follow it before a vowel, or if it's followed by only a single consonant that marks the end of the word (etch, en). Some letters make no sound at all, such as the silent "e" on the end of many words (slate, life). Some letters make different sounds when combined with other letters, as, for example, when "g" and "h" are combined and pronounced either as an "f" (rough, tough), or as if the "h" wasn't there (ghost), or perhaps as if neither letter was there (taught, fought). The combination "ough" can be pronounced in at least 6 different ways, "uf," as in the word "tough," "oo" as in the word "through," "off" as in the word "cough," "oh" as in "dough," "aw," as in "thought," and "ow" as in "bough."

The letters "c" and "x" have absolutely no reason to exist in English at all – "c" sounds like either "s" or "k" and could be replaced by them everywhere it appears, and "x" sounds like either "z" or "ks," and also needn't exist on its own. "Th" has both a hard and a soft form and so denotes two different sounds, and so does "ch," which sometimes sounds like "sh." Crazy, right?
A poem often attributed to American poet Charles Follen Adams but of unknown origin pokes quite clever fun at the state of affairs in trying to spell in English:

If an S and an I and an O and a U
With an X at the end spell Su;
And an E and a Y and an E spell I,
Pray what is a speller to do?
Then, if also an S and an I and a G
And an HED spell side,
There's nothing much left for a speller to do
But to go commit siouxeyesighed.

So the poor child having to learn to read English has to figure out which of the many sounds a given letter could make is the one it's supposed to make in this particular word. Spelling of some words, such as "maintenance," "occasion," "independence," "accommodate," and "argument," give people fits for a lifetime. And what do you do about the triple homophones of "there," "their," and "they're," not to mention "two," "too," and "to?"

How much easier would it be if there was only one spelling form for all three uses?

Now contrast this state of affairs with some other languages. Many languages are totally phonetic. Russian is an excellent example--every letter makes one and only one sound. So if you can pronounce a word correctly in Russian, you can spell it correctly as well, because only one spelling is possible for those sounds. Conversely, if you run across unfamiliar words in Russian, you can read them and pronounce them even if you don't know what they mean. Imagine how much simpler it is for young children to learn to spell simple words Russian, and how many more complex words a Russian schoolchild can spell in comparison with the poor child trying to spell in English! Other written languages are often between these two extremes – they're not as strictly phonetic as Russian, but most don't begin to be the phonetic nightmare that English is. The fact that languages differ in this fundamental way makes comparison of the average reading and spelling skills of children speaking two different languages very much equivalent to comparing the average size of apples and grapefruit.

When it comes to other aspects of English as a tool of intellectual adaptation, it fares better on some issues, and worse others. Let's move on to grammar, another important aspect of linguistic expression. The grammatical rules of verb conjugation in English aren't too bad on the surface of things. If you did a task in the past, you add "-ed" to the verb, if you are currently doing it, you add "ing," as in "I *worked* there yesterday, and I'm *working* there today." You have to go back to the unconjugated form and add an auxiliary to talk about the future, saying, "I *will work* tomorrow." That seems straightforward enough, and it is for the regular verbs. But English abounds in irregular verbs. If we're talking about the word "see," for example, we can say we're "seeing" it now, but we can't say we "seed" it yesterday. Instead, the correct form is "saw" for no particular reason other than that it's always been that way. If we're talking about the word "go," we can say that we are "going" but not that we "goed." Some of the most commonly used words in English, the verbs of being and doing and having, are all irregular, and often in different ways. You can say you're "seeing" things, "doing" things, and "going" places, but you can't say "I *having* a folder," or even "I am *having* a folder," but must use the unconjugated "I *have* a folder" instead. And the past tenses aren't always regular, either. If you're playing checkers and make it to the other end of the board, you can say that your opponent "kinged" you, but if he takes exception to your style of play and flattens you with a punch you can't say he "ringed" your bell, because the proper past tense of "ring" is "rung." But a person executed with a noose is said to be "hanged," not "hung." Plurals are just as silly. The plural of "dog" is "dogs," and the plural of "cat" is "cats." But the plural of "mouse" is "mice," the plural of "goose" is "geese," and the plural of "moose" is, well, "moose." The plural of "foot" is "feet," but the plural of "coot" is "coot," and the plural of "root" is "roots." The plural of "hoof," though, is "hooves."

So how in the world did you ever learn to read and write and conjugate in English? Through memorization, mostly, and years of practice. In addition, you learned English before your brain conducted inventory in your early teens and then went about wiping out redundant and unnecessary neural connections, making it faster and more efficient but less able to easily adapt to such nonsense afterward.

Other languages aren't immune from unnecessary silliness, either, and some have their own brands of silliness. One ridiculous adornment that English lacks, and many other languages have, is a complicated little fiasco known as "gender." In English, we have different pronouns for things that are masculine, feminine, and neuter, but they only apply to things that also have a sex. So things that are male are referred to as "he" or "him," things that are female are referred to as "she or her," and everything else is referred to as "it." Verbs don't change at all, regardless of the gender of the subject, and neither do adjectives. We only have three articles in English, "the," "a" and "an," and we use all three for all three genders. "The" is used if we're referring to a specific thing, "a" if we're referring to an indefinite thing that starts with a consonant, and "an" if we're referring to a thing that starts with a vowel or a vowel sound.

Compared to some other languages, that's incredibly straightforward and simple. In a lot of other languages many things have a gender that don't have a sex. You have to know the gender of these things in order to speak about them, and you have to use the correct articles and the correct pronouns for masculine or feminine items when you speak about them. For example, in German, the word for car, *wagen*, is masculine, so if we were talking about a specific car we'd use the German definite article, "der" to refer to it, as in "der Wagen." But the word for automobile is "auto," and in German it's neuter, so they say "das Auto." The sun is feminine "die Sonne," but the moon is masculine "der Mond." These genders often make no sense at all, and vary from language to language. In Spanish, in contrast to the above, the moon is feminine and the sun is masculine. Germans refer to their homeland as masculine, hence "der Vaterland," or "the Fatherland" but Russians consider it feminine, using the word "Rodina," meaning, literally, "the Motherland" (The use of a capital letter for Rodina tells us it's "the" motherland. Use of a small letter would mean "a" motherland).

I know what you're asking. Do all languages have to be this complicated? We know they don't, because there are perfectly functional languages lacking each one of these features. But humans apparently love the unnecessary complication of our languages, or at least we don't despise it, because we burden most of our languages with at least some of these features. This very fact makes it hard to compare reading, writing, and language abilities across cultures, because some tasks are harder in some languages, and some tasks are harder in others. If the average child in one culture can express himself better in his language than the average child in another culture, is that because of the children's abilities, or because of the differences in the language? Your guess is as good as mine. Then add to the mix the fact that differences in the variances of abilities from one culture to the other, and the question of what causes of differences in averages, or whether differences in averages mean anything, both become hopelessly complex.

Averages and the Battle of the Sexes

Another average difference you've probably heard about, and that people give more credence than they probably should, is ability differences in verbal skill between males and females. You've probably heard your whole life that the average female is better at verbal skills than the average male (Hyde, 1981). So if I stand a 10-year-old boy and a 10-year-old girl in front of you and ask which one has better verbal skills, your best bet is to pick the girl, right?

No, you're not going to fall for that one, are you? We're back to talking about averages again, in this case probably the mean or the median, and you know better than to assume that either average represents very many people. I could very well have picked a boy from the top of the verbal ability distribution and a girl from the middle of it just to confound you. Even if I pick the kids right from the middle of the distribution, a boy with the median score for boys and a girl with the median score for girls, we still might not be able to say which sex scored higher in which ability. Our means and the medians may both be misleading.

It all goes back to our old friend the variance again. The variance in verbal skills of boys, for example, is wider than the variance of verbal skills of girls, because there are more boys with what are called "verbal disabilities," or serious problems in learning verbal skills. This occurs for a number of reasons. First, boys tend to have more birth complications such as oxygen deprivation during birth than girls, because they tend to be bigger and heavier fetuses with bigger heads. Such complications often affect intellectual abilities like verbal skills. Second, girls have more genetic redundancy, or backup for their genes. Both sexes have 23 pairs of chromosomes. You got one full set of 23 chromosomes from your mother and one full set of twenty-three chromosomes from your father. Twenty-two of these are called autosomes, and they're homologous to each other, meaning that the corresponding chromosomes from each parent carry genes for the same functions in making particular proteins (though different versions of the genes make variants of each protein). And for females, the 23rd pair is like that, too, with a gene on each chromosome that has the same purpose as the corresponding gene on the matching chromosome. So little Esmeralda has two of these large, matching chromosomes, chromosomes that are commonly known as X chromosomes.

Esmeralda's brother Lutwidge, on the other hand, is a boy, and thus he only has one of these big X chromosomes. The other chromosome, obtained from his dear father Lutwidge the Elder, is a little tiny chromosome only a fraction of the X chromosome's size, with virtually none of the X chromosome's genes on it, a tiny chromosome known as the Y chromosome. (Most people notice that X chromosomes resemble the letter X, and mistakenly assume the Y chromosome got its name because it resembles the letter Y. It actually doesn't – it resembles a letter X in shape, like all the other chromosomes. The X chromosome was called "X" because it was unusual compared to other chromosomes in not having a matching partner in males. The Y chromosome was then called a "Y" chromosome, not because it looks like a letter Y, but because Y is the letter after X in the alphabet.)

You probably learned in 5th grade biology that some genes are dominant and some are recessive. Dominant genes are genes that show up if at least one of them is present, whereas recessive genes are not visible if the person also has a dominant gene for that trait. So if a person inherits a gene for brown eyes, that person will have brown eyes even if the other gene on the corresponding chromosome from the other parent is for blue eyes, because brown is dominant over blue. The only way for a person to have blue eyes is if he or she has nothing but genes for blue eyes on both chromosomes.

A lot of recessive genes are recessive because they are actually mutations of another gene, mutations that make them fail to make the protein the other gene makes. For example, blue-eyed people are actually blue eyed because they don't make a functional enzyme that normally turns the blue pigment in the iris of the eyes brown, probably because both genes they have for that purpose are mutated. Brown eyes is dominant because if you have even one gene that makes a functional enzyme, all the blue pigment will be turned to brown and you'll have brown eyes.

Now let's look at the sex chromosomes. The X chromosome is much larger than the Y and carries a whole slew of genes that the Y chromosome doesn't carry and thus doesn't back up. So males like Lutwidge have no backup for those genes if the gene on their sole X chromosome is defective.   Such genes are called "sex-linked," and even when they're recessives they show up in males if they're present, simply because there is no corresponding gene on the Y chromosome and thus no chance of the recessive gene hiding under it. But in females such recessive genes usually aren't visible, because they're masked by a dominant gene on the other X chromosome.

It's fairly likely that at least some of the genes on the X chromosome play roles in intellectual ability, or interact with genes that do. The genes that help us to learn language by making some helpful or needed protein would likely be dominant, and thus defective genes would be recessive. In females, there's a backup chromosome for the X, and thus a recessive on that chromosome that makes language learning harder would probably be hidden and cause no harm. But in males, such nasty recessives would show, because males have no backup for defective X chromosome genes. The net result is more males with X-linked genetic disabilities than females, and some of those disabilities may affect verbal skill.

So consider what might happen to the mean verbal abilities of boys vs. girls as a result of these two factors that afflict more boys than girls. If there are more males with verbal disabilities than girls, that would pull the mean of males down substantially. It would do so even if the rest of boys and girls, excluding those with verbal disabilities, were identical in ability. It would pull the mean down even if the medians for both sexes were identical. Yet that's not the impression most people get when they see the means of verbal abilities. They assume that this means that girls have higher verbal ability across the entire distribution, not realizing that the greater variance for the boys may be responsible for a big part of the difference.

This is a case where it would make more sense to use the median as the appropriate average rather than the mean. The median isn't as susceptible to being affected by outliers on one end of the distribution who score far lower than everyone else. But the median is seldom used in these verbal ability comparisons, most probably because the median isn't as different between males and females, and thus isn't as interesting.

Even putting the larger number of boys with reading disabilities aside, it's still very hard to compare verbal skills of males and females to each other. Our usual method is to give people standardized tests, or tests where everyone is given the same materials and follows the same procedures, after which we compare their scores. Most people would consider this a perfectly fair way to assess abilities, and to compare the sexes to each other. You give everyone the same materials and see who does better with them. But it's not that easy. You see, it matters which materials you use.

Say you want to test reading comprehension of 12-year-olds, and compare the boys to the girls. You want to give these children a passage of some complication to read, then ask them questions about the passage to determine whether they comprehended it. What reading passages should we use?

Here's a real shocker –12-year-old boys and girls have somewhat different tastes in reading. Sure, both boys and girls like Harry Potter (probably for slightly different reasons), but otherwise the overlap isn't that great. The boys prefer reading stories with more action in them, more violence, and more issues of dominance and conquest. The girls are more likely to prefer reading stories that involve the complex social relations between people, stories where the issues are trust and betrayal and rifts in the social fabric as well as, gasp, romance. The kids are interested in different subject matters, too, because boys and girls specialize in learning different hobbies and skills.

So, you say, we'll be fair and use standard reading course material from state approved reading textbooks in our tests. That's what's used in reading classes, you reason, so it should be familiar to all the kids, and fair to them all. Well, not exactly. The content of reading books for grade schools and middle schools tends to be materials of far greater interest to girls than to boys, and so, for many years, were the contents of standardized tests, giving the girls quite an edge when it came to standardized testing. This isn't a deliberate favoring of girls over boys by publishers or test designers. It's just the natural consequence of the process by which reading textbooks for schools are created.

The designers of reading and literature textbooks have a truly Herculean task. Most grade school and middle school reading books are designed to meet the approval of book selection committees of states and school districts across the nation. That means that anything that might offend more than a few people in more than a few states is unlikely to show up in such books. There's a pretty long list of the things that parents and school boards might be offended by. That list tends to include most of the things that boys prefer in their stories, including themes involving great amounts of violence and sex, themes of rebellion, examples of antisocial behavior, and extremely scary content such as vampires and werewolves. (We're not talking about sparkly vampires here, we're talking about bloodthirsty, rip-you-throat-out vampires.) So what kinds of plots and content are left? Pretty much all that's left are problems involving social rifts and stories of betrayals of trust, stories where violence doesn't succeed and sex is something that never comes up. For many boys, we end up with stories that just aren't all that interesting, yet many of the elements girls favor are still present. So if we use material from reading textbooks on our standardized tests, we're more likely to be testing using material of interest to girls rather than boys.

So can we compare the average reading abilities of boys and girls from standardized tests such as the ACT or the SAT? Again, such a comparison is probably less informative than it might first appear. Makers of standardized college admissions tests have, in fact, been systematically revising their tests over the last 20 years to remove reading material where males and females show differing average scores, and to include material where males and females score comparably. The net result of that is that differences in the verbal scores of males and females on tests like the SAT have been narrowing substantially during that period. But whether that means that the difference is narrowing because we're now testing young adults more accurately or it's narrowing because we're actually shifting the tests to give males an unfair advantage and hide their deficit compared to girls cannot be determined (Stanley, et al., 1992).

It's likely that in trying to protect our children, especially our boys, from the harsher aspects of the world, we've made reading less interesting and attractive to them. It's often not until high school that teens are allowed to explore the big themes of adult literature, violence and sex. By then, though, many boys have decided that they don't much care for reading. Parents often decry some of the popular books available for children. There are whole groups of parents denouncing *Harry Potter* for its graphic violence and its portrayal of fantasy magic and witchcraft. There are parents who deplore the "Captain Underpants" series, with its titles such as *Captain Underpants and the Invasion of the Incredibly Naughty Cafeteria Ladies from Outer Space (and the Subsequent Assault of the Equally Evil Lunchroom Zombie Nerds), Captain Underpants and the Attack of the Talking Toilets,* and *Captain Underpants and the Perilous Plot of Professor Poopypants.* There are those who campaign against the gross-out humor of *"How to Eat Fried Worms."* Judy Blume's *"Then Again, Maybe I Won't"* has been banned from libraries for even suggesting that pubertal boys might find looking at girls arousing, and the classic *Catcher in the Rye* has been accused by many of inciting adolescent angst and encouraging delinquent behavior. The modern craze of vampire love stories, currently being devoured by preteen and teen girls, have been condemned as the lowest sort of "soft-core horror porn." But all these books have been hugely successful, in part because they interest whole generations of kids of both sexes. Most kids also love graphic novels, generally referred to as "comic books" in the United States. Many parents deplore them, and say they don't want children reading such "trash," often objecting mostly to the violence that's common in most action comics, and the fact that pictures carry much of the story. But kids read them. When all of these "unacceptable" books are banned, many of those kids then read nothing at all.

Life Expectancy

Still, when it comes to being misleading, the above examples of misleading statistics don't even hold a candle to one of the most misunderstood averages of all time, life expectancy. You run into life expectancy everywhere. Insurance companies calculate them and base premiums on them, we use them as indicators of quality of life and health care in different countries, and you can even find online sites where you can feed your own data into a life expectancy calculator, which will then spit out the age to which you're theoretically supposed to live. Yet, almost nobody knows what average life expectancy really is, how it is calculated, and what it really means.

On the surface, the news about life expectancy is pretty encouraging. Estimated life expectancy rose steadily all through the 20th century and into the 21st, and that's got to gladden the little cockles of your heart (and who doesn't want glad cockles?). For example, life expectancy of the people of Massachusetts in 1785 was only 28, but by 1900 life expectancy in the United States was 45, and by 2005 it had risen to 77 (Coleman & Bond, 1990). (We're talking about combined life expectancy of both males and females here – mileage tends to be lower if you have the optional male equipment package, whereas mileage is higher if you go for the sportier female equipment package instead).

My students in classes like gerontology invariably look at these data, including the steady increase in life expectancy, and conclude that, by the time they're old, we'll be living routinely to 100, or even 120. Unfortunately, they're probably dead wrong, and I mean literally dead in this case. That's because gains in life expectancy involve gains in the average age people reach, not gains in the maximum age people reach.

Life expectancy of people of the past is easy to calculate. You just add up the dying age of every person who was born in a given year, and then you divide by the total number of people. This gives a mean, or average age. But how do you calculate the life expectancy of people who are still alive? Most of the time, the life expectancy of those still living is calculated by starting with the person's current age, and then estimating what percentage of people that age will make it to the next birthday by looking at how many people died during that year of their lives over the last few years. Then you calculate the odds they'll die the next year the same way, and the next, and you do that until the odds of dying each year, when added together, bring the total number of people expected to be dead to 50%. So what we're estimating is a sort median age of dying, the age that half of people will be dead. It's a complicated statistic, but it's probably our best guess of how many years you've get left if we know nothing about you, such as whether your ancestors were long-lived people or not.

But both of these statistics for calculating life expectancy are strongly susceptible to the death of newborns and infants. If 8 people live to be 80 and two die at birth, the mean age of the whole group is only 64, despite the fact that many of the people lived longer than that. Back in Massachusetts in 1785, more than a third of children died in infancy, and quite a few more died before reaching adulthood. The loss of that many infants and children pulled the mean lifespan down dramatically. But the majority of people who managed to survive the first few years of life often lived to be much older than the average age of 28.

This is where the bad news comes in for those of you planning to live to 120. The bulk of the increase in life expectancy since Colonial times has been due to lowering that formerly sky-high infant mortality rate, not in increasing the maximum age people reach. By 1900, with fewer infants dying after birth, life expectancy numbers climbed, and by the end of the 20th century, we'd reached the point where most babies, and indeed, most people, can expect to get somewhere near their genetically and biologically-limited maximum possible lifespan.

So increases in life span since Colonial times are primarily due to the fact that fewer people die before their time these days, with little due to actually lengthening the maximum lifespan. For many years, now, the verifiably oldest person in the world at any given time has been around 114, and that number never changes much even while lifespan has been increasing. Most of the problems that kill the very old are problems that are tough to crack, and that medical science doesn't have much of a chance of addressing anytime soon. The deterioration of the structure of membranes throughout the body, for example, means that old folks start having trouble keeping bacteria out of their blood and out of their brains once they get up into those high 70's and 80's. The deterioration of collagen, the binding molecule of the body that makes up tendons and holds in all our organs, is irreversible and inevitable as well. Arteries clog and stiffen, making strokes and heart attacks become more and more common until they're the norm. Cell mutation rates increase dramatically as cells get old, vastly increasing odds of tumors. We can slow these processes for awhile, and fight them when they occur, but we can't stop them.

What medical science can do is make it more likely we'll get the chance to live closer to our genetic potential by keeping things other than normal aging from killing us before our time. By doing so, it's raised life expectancy substantially. But most of us still only have about 80 or 85 good years in us, and many of us may not even have that many. That's because life expectancy averages are based on what is happening with today's old people. But there are several clouds on the horizon. Today's old people exercised more in their prime than the average younger person does today. They did more manual labor, they walked more often and for longer distances, and they ate less fat and fewer calories overall. They were less prone to obesity. All of these are factors that extend our chances of living to our maximum potential ages, and all of them are factors that are different now, and may shorten the maximum life spans of tomorrow's old people (that would be all of us). Because of this, life expectancy statistics may not just be giving us false hope, but might be allowing us to be dangerously complacent.

I can't end this book on a note that somber, so I'll end with a story instead. This involves a tough old gent who, on his 110th birthday, got a visit from his life insurance agent. The agent gave the man the sad news that his term life insurance policy won't be renewed because he had gotten too old. When the elderly gent asked why, the agent showed the man an actuarial table. The table had a column listing how many people were still alive out of 100,000 at each age, and the agent made his point by running a finger down the column, noting that by the age of 110 the number of people predicted to still be alive was 0. The old man took it rather well, in fact, he became downright gleeful. He patted the insurance man one the back, gave him a cigar, and sent him on his way. After the insurance man had left, the old man's family crowded around him. "Aren't you upset?" one of his elderly daughters asked. "He cancelled your insurance!"

"That doesn't matter," the old man replied gleefully. "Because he showed me a chart. After 110, nobody dies!"

Aw, come on! Statistics demonstrate that the average person loves that story!

References:

Coleman, P., & Bond, J. (1990). Aging in the twentieth century. In J. Bond & P. VColeman (Eds.), *Aging in society*. London: Sage.

Ge, X., Natsuaki, M. N., Neiderhiser, J. M., & Ross, D. (2007). Genetic and environmental influences on pubertal timing: Results from two national sibling studies. *Journal of Research in Adolescence, 17(4)*, 762-788.

Household Income Rises, Poverty Rate Unchanged, Number of Uninsured Down. (Retrieved 2010). Retrieved from http://www.census.gov/Press-Release/www/releases/archives/income_wealth/012528.html

Hyde, J. S. (1981). How large are cognitive gender differences? A meta-analysis using v² & d. *American Psychologist, 36*, 892-901. Miller, K. F., Smith, C. M., Zhu, J., & Zhang, H. (1995).

Preschool origins of cross-national differences in mathematical competence. *Psychological Science, 6*, 56-60.

No Country Left Behind. (Retrieved 2010). Retrieved from http://findarticles.com/p/articles/mi_qa3622/is_200501/ai_n94684 99/

Park, R. D., & Buriel, R. (1998). Socialization in the family: Ethnic and ecological perspecties. In W. Damon (Ed.), *Handbook of child psychology: Vol 3. Social emotional and personality development.* New York: Wiley.

Stanley, J. C., Benbow, C. P., Brody, L. E., Dauber, S., and Lupkowski, A. E., (1992). Gender differences on eighty-six nationally standardized achievement tests. In N. Coangelo, S. G. Assouline, & D. L. Ambroson (Eds.), *Talent Development.* Unionville, NY: Trillium.

ABOUT THE AUTHOR

Dr. Dean Richards grew up on a dairy farm near Columbus Junction, Iowa, but he left cold, damp winters and hot, humid summers behind forever after finishing graduate school. He now lives in Los Angeles with his lovely wife, Dr. Andrea Richards, enjoying periodic visits from their now grown children, generating almost all his own electricity from clean, silent solar panels, raising backyard tomatoes, working on the next volume of this series, and teaching psychology online as well as on site for a myriad of universities. He hopes you have enjoyed this volume of essays on psychology, and if so, he invites you to read the other volume in this series, *More Psychology in Plain English*, (provided you have not done so already). Both this volume and that one are available in paperback and for Kindle and Kindle Reader Apps on Amazon.com.

Dean enjoys hearing from readers, and appreciates online reviewers. If you'd like to contact him, you can do so at this email address:

deanrichardsbooks@gmail.com

Reviews can be posted for this volume on its web page on Amazon.com. The Amazon Kindle app for smartphones, tablets, and desktop computers can also be downloaded from Amazon.com. If you liked this book, please recommend it to a friend, or order a copy through Amazon to give as a lovely gift! Heck, order 10— shipping costs are much cheaper if you do!

CPSIA information can be obtained at www.ICGtesting.com
Printed in the USA
LVOW071959271212

313486LV00029B/1369/P